BRITAIN IN OLD PH(

BRADWELL
PAST & PRESENT

MARION HILL

SUTTON PUBLISHING LIMITED

Sutton Publishing Limited
Phoenix Mill · Thrupp · Stroud
Gloucestershire · GL5 2BU

First published 1998

Title page: Members of Old Bradwell Cricket
Club near the Prince Albert pub in the village,
c. 1910 (MKM). The wagonette was owned
and driven by Mr Derricott.

British Library Cataloguing in Publication Data

A catalogue record for this book is available from the
British Library.

ISBN 0-7509-1764-4

Typeset in 10/12 Perpetua.
Typesetting and origination by
Sutton Publishing Limited.
Printed in Great Britain by
Ebenezer Baylis, Worcester.

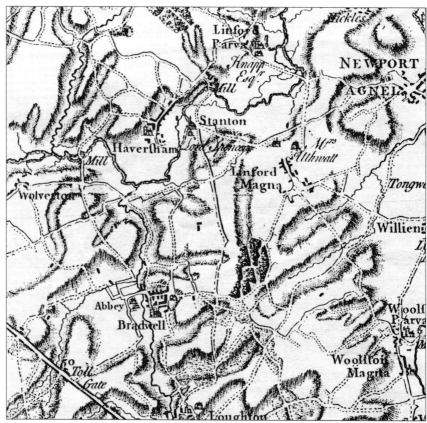

A 1788 map of the Bradwell parish area (BCC). The railway 'new towns' of Wolverton and New Bradwell
are still three-quarters of a century away. However, the deserted medieval village of Stanton is still shown,
on land owned by Lord Spencer – the family of the late Diana, Princess of Wales. Bradwell, still connected
to its abbey, is the most substantial community outside Newport Pagnell. The Toll Gate is on the ancient
Roman road, Watling Street – the A5. The dotted lines denote paths or tracks rather than roads.

CONTENTS

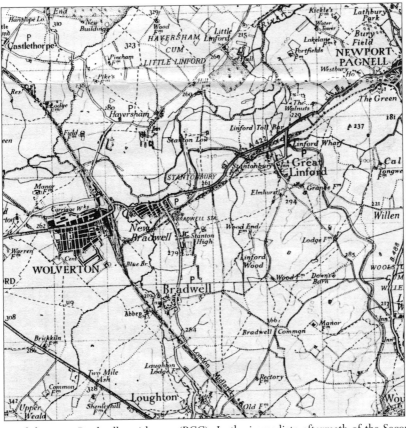

A 1946 map of the same Bradwell parish area (BCC). In the immediate aftermath of the Second World War, before Milton Keynes was even thought of, this map shows the dominance of the two railway communities of Wolverton and New Bradwell and a transformation of the transport system with new roads, railways and the canal. Stantonbury is prominent, despite its lack of residents. Several names adopted for new city estates 30 years later feature in this map.

Aerial view of the ruins of St Peter's Church, once part of the medieval village of Stanton Low, 1967 (J.E. Jennings, BCC). The village site is about 1½ miles north-east of New Bradwell, directly east of Haversham and just south of the modern Stantonbury Lake. The edge of the gravel pits can be seen at the top of the picture; the ruins of the church are between the two lone trees (centre and left) and can still be reached via the tow-path by the Grand Union Canal. The Stanton Manor House site was at the top left of the picture.

INTRODUCTION

The name of Bradwell covers perhaps one of the most confusingly labelled and disparate geographical areas in the new city of Milton Keynes: New Bradwell was created over 150 years ago, yet locals continued to call it Stantonbury until well into the 1930s, even though the village of Stanton itself ceased to function nearly 400 years before that; Old Bradwell assumed its venerable title only in the 19th century – even though it dates from Domesday times – and dropped it again in the 20th century when it became incorporated into the grid square system of Milton Keynes; and despite the many 'wells' recorded in the village, locals have stubbornly called it 'Braddle'; Bradville was named after the Cadbury's Bournville estate, while Bancroft, a Roman site, recalls a medieval bean field, and Blue Bridge a 19th-century railway construction; and despite their names, Bradwell Abbey is a prime industrial development in the city and Bradwell Common a large and popular housing estate.

The whole area is intersected by the ancient Bradwell Brook, crossed by Roman tracks, dissected by the 18th-century Grand Union Canal, sliced by the 19th-century London–Birmingham railway, and newly sectioned by the late 20th-century city grid-road system – the vertical bisection, north to south, of Grafton Street (V6) and the horizontal ones, west to east, of Millers Way (H2), Monks Way (H3), and Dansteed Way (H4).

However, in these same physical divisions and labels lie the historical secrets which unite them. More than any other area of Milton Keynes, Bradwell shows evidence of the history of England since the earliest settlers: from the fragments of Bronze Age implements of the New Bradwell area of 2000 BC to the disused Wolverton–Newport Pagnell railway branch line threading its modern route as a cycle redway; and from the remnants of pre-Milton Keynes life, like the 1930s Bradville, to the futuristic prototypes of housing, as in Bradwell Common's 'Homeworld '81'.

With the new millennium approaching, the temptation to pause and reflect a little on the past is unashamedly offered in this book. Although some of the older photographs themselves may have existed for little more than 100 years, the pictures bear witness to nearly 4,000 years of local life. They are accompanied by details collected from numerous sources: the marvellous newspaper archives at Milton Keynes Museum of Rural and Industrial Life; the unique Kitchener glass plate negatives held by the City Discovery Centre; the vast photographic archive compiled by the Commission for New Towns and Milton Keynes Development Corporation; the excellent Buckinghamshire County Council Libraries in Aylesbury and Central Milton Keynes; but perhaps more importantly, from the most precious and interesting source of all – that of human memory. I am particularly indebted to The Living Archive for giving me access to the transcripts of interviews recorded with local residents, the memories of whom span the whole of this century.

Browse and enjoy!

Marion Hill

A famous view of the Loughton Road approach to Old Bradwell, looking south, *c.* 1910 (BCC).

The same view, 1997 (MH). Nearly nine decades later, only the road layout, the trees and the form of transport seem to have changed.

CHAPTER ONE

OLD BRADWELL

An aerial view of Old Bradwell Village, looking south, 7 June 1983 (CNT). Loughton Road is on the left; Primrose Road runs across the bottom; Abbey Road is on the right; and Vicarage Road is just above the centre where housing development is taking place on the site of the old Nurseries.

Old Bradwell, as it has been known since 1840, is one of 13 villages incorporated into the new city of Milton Keynes. Its name comes from the Anglo-Saxon 'brad' (broad) and 'wella' (spring), so perhaps it is not surprising that the site shows evidence of having been occupied for over 1,000 years.

Domesday Book of 1086 refers to Bradewelle in the Hundred of Buckinghamshire of Seckloe or Sigelai – Warriors Hill. Indeed, the very ownership of the Bradwell parish seems to have emanated from conflict. For example, one of the medieval owners of the land, Walter Giffard, was Lord of Longueville in France, and a kinsman of William the Conqueror. Having furnished William with 30 ships for the invasion of England, and as commander of the Norman army at Hastings, he was rewarded with more manors than anybody outside the king's immediate family – nearly a sixth of the entire county of Buckinghamshire. In the Milton Keynes area, he owned estates in the Woolstones, Loughton, Linford, Broughton, Milton Keynes Village and Bradwell. Two centuries later in 1324, Henry II gave the Bradwell estate to the 'family of Keynes' as a reward for taking King Stephen prisoner. Three centuries after that, in the Civil War, the then Lord of the Manor, Sir Thomas Longueville, nailed his colours firmly to the Royalist mast and was heavily fined by the Roundheads for his trouble once they won power.

The old village was essentially a square of four roads – Loughton, Vicarage, Primrose and Abbey Roads – lined with dwellings surrounding an unbuilt core, a common feature of the area. Domesday Book records 16 men living in the village (women were not registered). By 1563 there were 16 'house lords', and by 1676 there were 212 residents. However, it was not until 1778 that the village appeared on maps of the area: until then, the nearest habitation was marked as Staunton – the site of Stanton High, now modern Bradville. Ten years later, the 1788 Enclosure Act caused great upheaval for villagers: 1,000 acres were enclosed by the owners, leaving just 22 acres of common land at the ancient site of Secklow (now Bradwell Common), and 15 acres 'for the poor in lieu of common right'. The 1798 *Posse Comitatus* (a partial census) records 37 families, most of whom were labourers. Others included four stone-masons, two cordwainers (shoemakers), a ratcatcher and a 'haggle cartman' – the only travelling salesman in the Newport area!

In 1838 the new railway divided the village from Bradwell Abbey. Osborne's *London and Birmingham Railway Guide* of 1840, which describes the journey from Euston Grove in London to Birmingham, mentions Bradwell, albeit briefly: 'On the right is the village and church of Bradwell, and close to the line is a quarry, from which materials have been taken to construct the neighbouring embankments.'

By 1864 the village had a shoemaker, carpenter, blacksmith, butcher, shopkeeper, two beer retailers and four farmers, one of whom was a baker. At the end of the century, when 493 people lived in the village, there were three pubs, a grocer, a post office, a blacksmith and a baker. Before 1919, when its links with New Bradwell were severed, the parish covered 917 acres, 85 per cent of which was devoted to agriculture – wheat, oats, barley and beans. The estimated Bradwell population in 1989, including its new city dwellers, was 3,080.

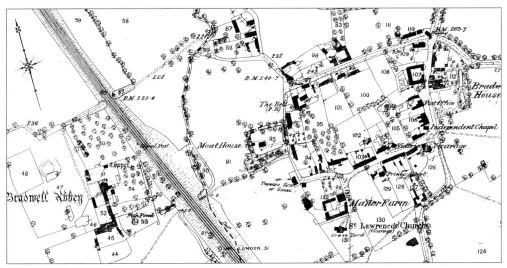

Map of Old Bradwell Village showing the first proposed site of a new school at the west end of Vicarage Road, *c.* 1880 (MKM). Loughton Road marks the eastern boundary of Old Bradwell. It used to continue north, as Bradwell Road in New Bradwell, a connection now severed by Monks Way (H3). At the top of the road on the west side was the Infants' School, built by the London and North Western Railway (LNWR) Company in 1891 to accommodate 60 children. The old school had closed in 1876, forcing children to walk a mile into New Bradwell. 'The road being a very bleak one, it was felt to be a great hardship for the infants' (*Bucks Standard,* 1891).

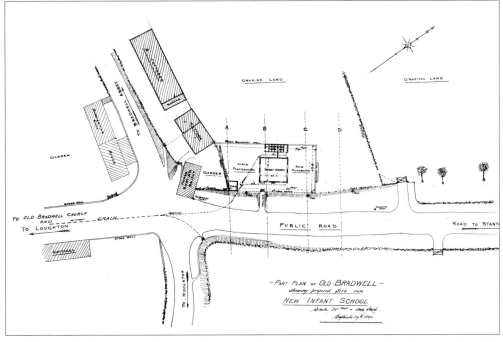

Final plan of school site on Loughton Road, 19 September 1890 (MKM). Originally, plans were drawn for sites near both St Lawrence's Church and the Prince Albert pub. The school finally opened on its Loughton Road site with 44 children under the supervision of Miss Stracey. The ubiquitous Mr Bird was the contractor. In 1957 the school closed, again requiring village children to travel to New Bradwell.

The old London and North Western Railway Infants' School, 1997 (MH). The building is now a private residence.

The old blacksmith's house and shop, 1997 (MH). On the corner with Primrose Road, opposite the school, was the old horse-shoeing smithy. Over the years at least two village blacksmiths were also teachers at the local Methodist Sunday School: Richard Wooton (1879) and Harold Nutt (1905).

The Old Vicarage (left) and Methodist Chapel (right), 1997 (MH). The Old Vicarage, built in the early 19th century, was valued in 1861 at £280, when *Sheahan's Guide* described it as 'a genteel residence'. An infants' school used to operate here 'entirely supported by Mrs Randolph', the vicar's wife. The Methodist Chapel, which Sheahan called 'small and neat', opened in 1823 as a venue for 'dissenting religion' and included a Sunday School for 16 children. In 1924 it was registered for marriages, and became renowned for its concerts, magic lantern shows and even a small library. Electric lights arrived in 1933, although worshippers had to wait until 1963 for heating.

A Scouts' gathering in Providence Place close to the Methodist Chapel, *c.* 1930 (WDAS). There had been a 'preaching station' in the village, initiated by Revd William Bull of Newport Pagnell, since the 18th century. Although the chapel itself had gone through a period of some disuse during the 19th century, by the 1880s there had been an active Methodist following in the village with as many as 44 children enrolled in the school. By 1973 there were only three ageing members of the chapel left, but with the help of the Bradwell parish churches, the 1980s brought new life, especially to its floor whose original wooden tiles had been laid directly on the soil!

Listed thatched cottages in Loughton Road, *c.* 1930 (WDAS). Further south on the road, just past these two 17th-century thatched cottages and opposite the site of the old village post office at Providence Place, is the early 18th-century Bradwell House.

Bradwell House, 1907 (WDAS).

Bradwell House, 13 September 1971 (CNT). A listed building with a notable staircase, Bradwell House is regarded as an excellent example of the early Georgian period, although it is thought by some to be an extension to a much earlier building. It was first occupied by Joseph Baily but its subsequent owners were the Selby Lowndes family, until 1939. The early 19th-century stables in the south wing of the yard and the diaper brick garden wall are also listed.

The house and grounds were often the focal point for village life: the Bradwell Sewing Meeting Class had their annual garden sale and fête there with such delights as the baby competition, hoopla, wicket dice, skittles, treasure island, bran tub, jumble stall, 'fancy and needlework' stall, balloon stall, square game, shooting range, tea and refreshments.

However, village life was not always so comfortably parochial: the First World War had an enormous effect on such communities throughout the land. The family at a nearby house, 11 Loughton Road, must have felt some relief and pride at the news they received in August 1917: Sgt Arthur Townsend was awarded the Military Medal for the sort of action dreamed of by generations of little boys of all ages: 'All the officers being killed or wounded, he took command of the Company, rallied it on the enemy's side of the ravine and finally withdrew it in the most difficult circumstances.'

During the Second World War, the house was used as a rest home for London firemen.

The Victoria Inn, *c.* 1950 (WDAS). Next to 4 Vicarage Road, a listed 18th-century cottage with a noted doorcase, is the Victoria Inn, a listed building itself, possibly from the 17th century. Before it became a pub, it seems to have been Newman's Farm, mentioned in a property sale dated 27 February 1639. The *Harrods Guide* of 1876 lists E. Bird as the landlord.

The Victoria Inn, 1997 (MH). At a 'Smoking Concert' of the Conservative Association held at the Victoria in June 1892, Farmer Wylie recalled having given his first vote to Disraeli in 1860 when there were only 20 voters for Bradwell: now, he said, there were 600. Later that year, the pub hosted the Annual Dinner of the village cricket club, for 40 guests. Charles Sambrook had somewhat different memories: 'All the bellringers went to the Victoria', he recalled.

Vicarage Road looking towards Loughton Road, *c.* 1905 (WDAS). The group of children at the top of the road are outside the Victoria Inn. Mr Foxley, a haberdasher from Loughton, stands with his cart outside the shop kept by Miss Coe.

A similar view, *c.* 1935 (WDAS). The Victoria Inn sign can be seen on the left, with the Prince Albert pub sign on the right.

The Church Mission tent in Old Bradwell, 1934 (WDAS). This was an annual event in Bradwell.

The bus-stop outside the Prince Albert pub, *c.* 1950 (WDAS).

The Prince Albert pub, 1997 (MH). The Prince Albert Public House, opposite the Victoria, is a listed early 19th-century building with a doorcase and fanlight of 'a more modern replacement'. On a 1900 map, it is not shown as a pub, although the 1876 *Harrods Guide* lists L. Pangbourne as landlord.

The east end of Vicarage Road and Old Sugar Loaf, *c.* 1905 (WDAS). On the corner of Alexandra Court, the listed cottage (no. 1), now known as Old Sugar Loaf (centre), is believed to be late 17th century, and possibly had a dairy at the rear. Further along the road is the Prince Albert (right). The triangle of grass (bottom) was removed in 1964. The extreme left leads to the modern bungalow development of Vicarage Gardens. Among the many vicars of Bradwell through the centuries are the splendidly named Henricus Capellanus of 1223; and the 'remarkably handsome' Revd Kitelee Chandos-Baly, who served for a record 52 years.

Vicarage Gardens (left) and Old Sugar Loaf (centre), 1997 (MH). The Revd Mr Eyles of Bradwell was considered by the diarist Revd William Cole to be 'the most notorious Gossip in the County, a Widower with a singularly unpromising Son of a rakish disposition!' (June 1766). Notwithstanding, Mr Cole himself relates Mr Eyles's gossip with the relish of a modern 'soap' fan! 'He told me a Deal of Scandal of other People . . . that Goodwin lay with Mrs. Holt; that Mrs. G told Frank that her Husband lay in the same Bed with her for three weeks together and never touched her; that Mr. Knapp and his Wife lived very unhappily; that they neither spoke to one another nor bedded together for some time; that the Widow Woods was a kept mistress. . . .'

Laying the Memorial Hall foundation stone, *c.* 1924 (WDAS).

The WI outside the Memorial Hall, 24 March 1965 (MKM). The Memorial Hall itself, at the west end of Vicarage Road, lists some well-known local names – those who died in action also featuring on the New Bradwell memorial. Five members of the Foolkes family alone went to war in 1914, one of them, Frank, losing his life. Another who 'also served' was James Wooton, relative of Arthur who came to local attention in 1891 when he organised a search party for a local man missing for three weeks. The *Bucks Standard* dramatically recorded how the five young men scoured the River Ouse until they found him 'floating in the stream'.

Memorial in New Bradwell cemetery (MH). In March 1917, Mr and Mrs Walters who lived at 9 Vicarage Road received the news dreaded by all families then – that their son had been killed in action. His Commanding Officer, 2nd Lt Piggott, wrote of him: 'He was killed instantly by a piece of shell. . . . He was my servant, an excellent servant, and his loss will not only be a great loss to me but to the Company to which he belonged.'

He ended with a grim illustration of how soldiers of the Great War – and their place of death – often simply vanished in the slaughter of the trenches: 'It may be some consolation to you that his grave is marked and his rifle laid out on it. . . .'.

The Bradwell motte, with the Memorial Hall top left, October 1981 (CDC/CNT). The village's earliest remains are of a Norman motte and bailey castle, south-west of the Prince Albert pub, just off Church Lane. Many pottery fragments have been found around the Memorial Hall grounds.

The Bradwell Manor Farmhouse, October 1981(CNT). Opposite the motte, the 17th-century Manor Farmhouse, now a youth hostel, was originally thatched with a 'nag' house, 'gig' house, pig house, hen house, carthorse stable, 'chaff' house, granary and drying kiln.

St Lawrence's Church, Old Bradwell, October 1981 (CDC/CNT). St Lawrence's Church was given to the Priory of St Mary at Tickford in Newport Pagnell over 700 years ago, in 1275. A listed building originating mostly from the 13th century, its 'saddleback' roof was incorporated into the rebuilding of the church in 1646. Its churchyard gate, along with the village pump, was built at the famed local iron works of E. and H. Roberts of Deanshanger in 1821.

St Lawrence's Church, c. 1900 (WDAS). *Kelly's Directories* of 1864 called the church 'an ancient edifice', and noted in 1887 that it had been restored in 1868. Although comfortably familiar, this early picture reveals some interesting changes over the years: an extra window has been added on the right; the door (left) and the railings (right) have been removed; the ugly chimney in the centre has been replaced by a cross; a lean-to boiler house was added on the side (left), then enlarged, then reduced to its present modest size; and extra drainpipes and new roofing ensure the church will endure still longer.

Bell hanging at St Lawrence's Church, Old Bradwell, 1909 (WDAS). Nineteenth-century tourists were urged to pause on their travels to see the church: the *Sheahan Guide* of 1861 described it as 'an ancient and venerable structure. . . . Its tower contains four bells' – of which the villagers were justly proud. The picture above shows the rehanging of the four bells along with two more made by A. Bowell of Ipswich. The bellhangers are, left to right: Charlie Bird, Tom Walters, Revd K.C. Bailey, Tommy Cook, George Walters, Arthur Wooton and Zach. Walters.

At the back of the church, the tombs of the Battam family have been recently discovered. For generations, they lived at Stacey Hill Farm – now the home of the MK Museum of Industry and Rural Life, where staff are currently researching the family's involvement in cross-country racing: they seem to have been an important influence in the history of the sport.

St Lawrence's Church interior, 1965 (MKM). The interior of the church is primarily of the late 12th century. Indeed, in its early days, the church was the site of a local drama when, according to the law-court records of 1227: 'Adam de Bradewell killed Robert Le Marchaunt and fled to the Church and abjured the realm.' He was subsequently captured, tried and hanged. (*Calendar of the Roll of the Justices of Eyre*, ed. J.G. Jenkins)

Most of Bradwell's new housing, developed by Milton Keynes Development Corporation and dating from 1978, is named after local celebrities who resided in the village over the last 850 years. John Platt is credited with much of the research for these names.

South of Old Bradwell
John Atte Brooke de Wiston was Vicar of Bradwell in 1361; the Hilliard family lived in the village in the 18th century; Thomas Sharman was recorded at Bradwell Abbey in 1728; Joseph Harcourt was a Bradwell resident in 1688; William Foster was vicar in 1533; Lady Catherine Maynard owned Manor Farm until her death in 1744; Henry Atkins was granted a pension from Bradwell Priory in 1624; John Travell was recorded a pauper in 1620, William Travell, a labourer in 1709; Hugh de Audeley, the Earl of Gloucester, died in 1348, 'holding Bradwell in service as morety of a knight's fee'; Thomas Bradbury was Vicar of Bradwell in 1173; William de Waldegrave was vicar in 1350; and Edward Haly was churchwarden in 1719.

North of Old Bradwell
Richard Rawlins was Bradwell's churchwarden in 1617; William Hampson was described as a 'gent of Bradwell' in 1619; John and Stephen Colley were recorded as residents in 1453; Simon de Ellenstow was Prior of Bradwell Abbey in 1331; and although Cardinal Wolsey was not a Bradwell resident, he was Henry VIII's powerful administrator following the split from the Roman Catholic Church and the subsequent dissolution of the monasteries. It was he who oversaw the Bradwell Abbey estate in 1526.

Atterbrook: a model of MKDC's 'Bradwell 8' scheme in 1982 (CNT).

Aerial view of Old Bradwell Village, 26 May 1965 (Aerofilms). Primrose Road (centre top) marks the northern edge of the old village. At its eastern junction with Loughton Road (right) is Common Lane which originally led to the Saxon Secklow meeting place, and later to the medieval hamlet of Stanton High: the bridle track still follows this ancient route.

Horace Felce was a resident of Primrose Road 50 years ago, and was one of two men killed on the railway at Wolverton in January 1947. The other was Jesse Millard of Spencer Street, New Bradwell. They were working the night shift as plate-layers. A witness described them walking along the line when they 'became enveloped in the smoke from a passing train'. Both were silently mown down by the express parcel train coming up behind.

More fortunate residents of the road were Mr and Mrs T. Bird, celebrating their Golden Wedding at Ivy House (no. 15) in 1937. 'Probably no couple is better known or held in higher esteem', said the local paper. Married at St Lawrence's in 1887, they lived in the village for 58 years. Mr Bird was a master builder (fourth generation) and was also the vicar's warden, sexton, parish clerk and foreman of the belfry. When he died, 5 years after his wife in 1947, it was in the same house in which he had been born 82 years before. Since 1948, Ray and Mary Bellchambers have lived in the house – 50 years.

Rear of Home Farm from King George V Recreation Ground, 1997 (MH). Along Primrose Road, past the old smithy's house, is the Recreation Ground, opened in 1937 after the Jubilee celebrations for King George V, and the well-known Home Farm with its inglenooks, timber frames and herring-bone roof – a village landmark since the 16th century.

Miss Ellen Tue, aged 28, shortly before she became Mrs Turner, wife of the nursery owner, in 1906 (WDAS). There are now 31 modern houses on the site of the old Nursery Gardens (centre of picture opposite). From here, in 1957, you could still buy spring cabbage plants for '6*d* a score'.

The Bradwell Stocks, *c.* 1900 (WDAS). The village stocks stood on the small 'godcake' green at the western end of Primrose Road – some say until the end of the 19th century; others insist they were still there in 1945! They were certainly among the last to survive *in situ* in the county. All agree that they were opposite the last house which was on the south corner with Abbey Road. In June 1905, a letter appeared in the *Wolverton Express* from Mr W.R. Beckwith who complained that a Dr Harvey had bought the stocks from the Parish Council for £2, because, he said, it had cost him that to clear away the rubbish when the tree on the green fell down. Subsequently, parish councillors decided to send a deputation of three to negotiate with the doctor for their return. It seems they were unsuccessful.

The site of the stocks, 1997 (MH). The new tree was planted for the Queen's Silver Jubilee in 1977 by Ray and Mary Bellchambers. Abbey Road is to the left, Primrose Road to the right. Home Farm, much photographed from this perspective, is here hidden by the trees – by the second lamp-post on the right.

The Bradwell Stocks and the Bell Inn (left), *c.* 1900 (WDAS). The house opposite the green used to be the Bell Inn, whose landlord in 1864 was William Shouler, and in 1876, W. White. The inn enjoyed rural customs, and customers, well into the next century. 'All the farmworkers went to the Bell' (Charles Sambrook). The Old Bradwell Annual Feast used to end there: with the Bradwell Band playing, the tables set out and drinks for all, it was 'a good old night!' (Hawtin Mundy).

The Bradwell May Queen, 1953 (WDAS). There would be fancy dress parades and sporting events restricted to residents of Old Bradwell and West View. Perhaps the young man who came second in the 100-yard race in 1927 was the same unfortunate railway employee who, 27 years later, was killed in an accident at the works a week before Christmas in December 1954: P. Rainbow.

Bradwell Fête on the Memorial Hall site, *c.* 1910 (WDAS).

The Bradwell Tennis Club Fête in 1935 (WDAS). The tennis courts used to be in Mr and Mrs Bird's orchard in the grounds of Ivy House.

Excavation of 'Castle Mound' near the Moat House, *c.* 1975 (WDAS). Along Abbey Road, the modern cricket pitch and sports field cover the ancient earthworks, known as Bradwell Bury – 'Braddlebury'. There were a manor house and outbuildings, including two circular dovecotes. Nearby is the 18th-century Moat House (1784), considered to be a good surviving example of a moated dwelling originating from medieval times. The *Sheahan Guide* of 1861 called it a 'good-sized comfortable cottage'.

The newly built Sports Club with the restored Brookfield cottages behind, *c.* 1975 (CDC/CNT).

Brookfield Cottages before restoration by MKDC, 1975–6 (CNT). House nos 1–4 Abbey Road are the 16th- and 17th-century Brookfield Cottages; the back garden of no. 1 has the original well. In fact, all Bradwell residents had to use well water until 1937. In June of that year, the roads were reported to be 'in turmoil' when pipes were laid 'in paths and roadways where houses lie'.

Brookfield Cottages, Abbey Road, 1997 (MH). Of course, the original function of the Abbey Road was to lead to Bradwell Abbey. It cannot do this directly today although, since the coming of the railway, there has been a special footpath under the line – now a cycle redway.

CHAPTER TWO

BRADWELL ABBEY &
BRADWELL COMMON

Aerial view, looking south, of Bradwell Abbey Manor House (centre) and 'Phase 3 Industry' (right), 7 June 1983 (CNT). The Bradwell Brook can be seen emerging from under the railway, left. It followed its re-routed channel rather reluctantly, however, and later caused a slippage in the embankment on regaining its traditional course.

Over 800 years ago, in 1155, when Bradwell Village had already been home to at least six generations of residents, a Benedictine priory was founded by Meinfelin, the Lord of Wolverton. All that remains now are its moat, fish ponds and a 14th-century Pilgrims' Chapel of St Mary (listed Grade I). The priory monks believed that the figure of the Virgin Mary in a niche on the west front of their church had miraculous healing qualities, so they enclosed the figure within the protective building of the chapel. Its wall paintings date from 1350, and its floor tiles are believed to be from Little Brickhill 600 years ago. By the turn of the last century, the chapel was described as 'now disused, and converted into a lumber store for farm purposes'. A whimsical entry in the *LMS Railway Route Book* of 1947 reads: 'Kindly nature had lent to this woeful ruin a sweet touch of symbolism, for the weed that appears to choke the window, visible from the train, is in truth, a wild vine.'

The site of Bradwell Abbey can claim a much older pedigree even than Old Bradwell Village: a 4th-century Romano-British defensive enclosure was found nearby, about a quarter-mile from Watling Street. Later, several notable families held the manorial rights of the estate, including William de Bayeux (12th century) and Peter Barre, or Barry (13th).

The priory suffered terribly from the Great Plague of 1349 when even its prior, William of Loughton, succumbed. By 1431, however, it was providing school dinners to 'some teachable children to be instructed in reading, song and other branches of knowledge'. By 1500, they were learning weaving and dyeing. In 1506, its reputation for holiness was somewhat marred by the action of the then prior and his monks when they forcibly enclosed 300 acres – the largest seizure at the time – and their 20 tenants were turned off the land. Perhaps it was unsurprising that when the monks were themselves ejected from their lands with Henry VIII's dissolution of the monasteries, they received little sympathy. In 1526, when the lands came under Cardinal Wolsey's control, they were valued at £53 11s 2d.

The 14th-century Chapel of St Mary at Bradwell Abbey, renovated by MKDC, February 1980 (CNT).

Aerial view of Bradwell Abbey grounds, *c.* 1980 (CNT). The outlines of the ancient abbey buildings can be seen on the left. The railway runs from centre right to the top of the picture, with the Bradwell Brook just above it. The construction of Monks Way (H3) is in process (top left). Alston Drive runs from the bottom of the picture to centre left. In 1666, the Bradwell estate was purchased by Sir Joseph Alston (Baron of Chelsea and Bradwell Abbey). He enlarged the Manor Farmhouse (centre), restored the chapel (above the farmhouse) and created a park 'with a fine avenue of trees' running west from the house. The Bletchley diarist of the 18th century, the Revd William Cole, however, dismissed the Alston family as 'half-mad'! The building is now listed Grade II along with its barns. The *Victoria County History*, written at the turn of the century, described how 'the Bradwell Abbey mansion contains some wainscoted, spacious and lofty rooms'. The 1947 *LMS Railway Route Book* again indulged in a little whimsy when it referred to the supposed ghost of the farmhouse: 'Along that avenue that marches sturdily up the slope away from the railway, there whisks on fateful nights a chariot whose occupant carries her head under her arm . . .'.

The 17th-century Bradwell Abbey Manor Farmhouse, February 1980 (CNT).

The 14th-century Bradwell Abbey Malt House,
13 September 1971 (CNT).

Aerial view of Bradwell Abbey industry, October 1980 (CNT). At the bottom of the picture above the A5D road are (left) the first of the advanced factory units (AFUs) and (right) workshop units. Bradwell Abbey Manor Farmhouse is centre right, with Old Bradwell Village and some of its new housing development above right. The Bancroft site is centre left and Bradville is top right. New Bradwell can just be seen top left.

In 1971, the Manor Farmhouse and Chapel were designated as the Bradwell Abbey Archaeological Field Centre, now known as the City Discovery Centre. The present industrial estate of AFUs – designed by MKDC – and of purpose-built premises was developed from 1980. By 1988, some 1,285 employees worked there.

Bradwell Common Housing, *c.* 1985 (CNT). In the days of King Alfred the Great, 1,200 years ago, the county divisions of England were composed of 'hundreds' – an area of land inhabited by about 100 households. The meeting place of each hundred was generally on high ground with a protective covering of trees. Here, justice was administered, property sales took place, and political issues were debated. The meeting place for the 'Sigelai' or Secklow Hundred, in which Old Bradwell Village was situated, was Bradwell Common.

Bradwell Common 'Homeworld '81', 30 May 1981 (see also p. 38). Probably two Roman roads or tracks crossed on Bradwell Common – one from modern Stantonbury through to Woughton, Simpson and Fenny Stratford, the other from Shenley across Watling Street through Loughton to Willen. The local centre was built in 1988 and originally included, appropriately enough, a meeting place, along with a combined school, local park, public house, take-away, hairdresser, baker, general store and clothes shop. The estimated population in 1989 was 2,360.

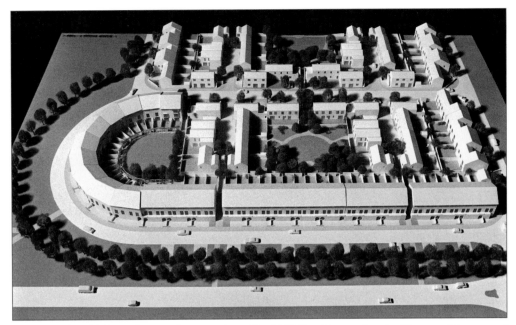

A 1979 model of 'Phase 1 housing for rent scheme' by MKDC architects, showing Plumstead Avenue and Blackheath Crescent (CNT). Since 1979, the modern Bradwell Common has been developed: the dwellings were designed largely by Martin Richardson (e.g. Plumstead and Wisley) and Edward Cullinan (e.g. Mitcham). They are in housing blocks measuring 150 × 100 metres.

Bradwell Common houses being built, March 1981 (CDC/CNT). The names of the roads are based on commons in London and Buckinghamshire. One of them, Brill Place, has a closer link with Bradwell: most of the pottery used in the area came either from Potterspury (north on the A5), or from one of the seven potteries of Brill in Buckinghamshire. It was characterised by brown earthenware, and plates, pots and jugs with a yellow or green glaze. The potteries were active from 1234 but closed down in 1870.

The 'Homeworld '81' Ideal Homes solar house (CDC/CNT). Coleshill Place is the site of a former housing exhibition called 'Homeworld '81', now privately occupied. Twenty architects and developers from five countries were invited by MKDC to design 36 dwellings, using at least one innovation, such as low-cost starter homes, A-framed houses, or solar houses. Among many innovative and individual designs were the Ideal Homes Solar (no. 5), Autarkic's Lead Harvester and Lead Cultivator (nos 29 and 30), the Money Programme 2000 (no. 4), and the Askeryd Pyramid (no. 36).

The Homeworld play area, May 1981 (CDC/CNT).

CHAPTER THREE

BANCROFT & BLUE BRIDGE

A Roman coin from the Bancroft and Blue Bridge excavations (CNT).

If Old Bradwell residents have a continued line from the 9th century AD, and the Bradwell Abbey estate had 4th-century inhabitants, those in the Bancroft area can claim forebears from nearly 1,500 years before!

Around the 9th century BC, a Bronze Age family began what would be nearly 3,000 years of continuous settlement of the area when they built a large circular timber house. However, Bancroft is nationally famous primarily for being the site of a Roman villa farm built on top of this earlier house, some 18 metres in diameter. It is the earliest known house in the Milton Keynes area and one of the largest of its kind in the country. It was discovered in 1971 by Denis Mynard near the Bradwell Brook and incorporated into the Linear Park by Milton Keynes Development Corporation. The excavations are some of the most extensive yet carried out on a Roman villa anywhere in the country.

The house was built in the 1st century AD – soon after Julius Caesar had successfully invaded Britain. The newly arrived settlers seem to have been impressed with what was on offer in their new location by their use not of imported materials but of local limestone to build the house. They seem to have been well-off, too: their house had a lavish bath suite which included a furnace room, hot room, warm room, cold-plunge room, and a bath lined in dark red waterproof concrete, and floored with red terracotta tiles. Also excavated were decorative painted murals, a granary, barns and a trackway.

By the 4th century AD, the descendants of, or successors to, these first Italian immigrants seem to have become even wealthier: formal gardens were laid around the house and included an ornamental pond, a summer-house, mosaics and wall paintings. (One of the mosaics can be seen on permanent display on the wall of Queen's Court in the Central Milton Keynes shopping building.) These residents left behind their coins, their jewellery, their pots, a board game in decorated limestone, even an old shoe, size 7½!

The Bancroft Villa Mosaic *in situ*, 1977 (Ron Unwin/WDAS). It is now on display at Queen's Court.

Visitors to the Roman Villa excavation site, September 1977 (CDC/CNT). Most of the road names on the Bancroft estate have Roman connotations. Bancroft itself is a local field name from about AD 1300 meaning 'land where beans are grown'. However, specialist flint tools for stunning birds and felling red deer have been found in the area, suggesting that neolithic hunters roamed around here 6,000 years ago!

Sketch of how the Bancroft Villa might have looked (CDC/CNT). The summer-house can be seen centre left, with the formal gardens bottom left.

The Bancroft Villa excavation site, September 1977 (CDC/CNT). The Bancroft area also covers a swathe of the Linear Park which, with its leisure paths, bridle trails and picnic sites, is an important resource for Milton Keynes citizens. It includes a 'wet/dry balancing lake' – part of the flood control system designed for the new city whereby low-lying areas along brooks and rivers are used for the storage of storm water after heavy rains; when dry, it is used as parkland and for animal grazing. Thus, the awesome floods of the '30s and '60s, when the otherwise benign Bradwell Brook caused havoc for residents, are now a thing of the past.

Aerial view of Bancroft, 7 June 1983 (CNT). The villa site is top left of the picture. Millers Way (H2) runs across the top right corner; Hadrians Drive is across the bottom right corner with Greatchesters, Haltonchesters and Richborough leading off from it; and the Bradwell Brook provides a curved spine to the North Loughton Valley Park across the top left corner.

Blue Bridge, looking west along H2 Millers Way (left) towards south Wolverton, a main line express passing underneath, 1997 (MH). Close to Bancroft is the famous Blue Bridge over the railway, its name taken from the distinctive blue bricks used to build it 160 years ago. The original bridge was to become 'a favourite spot for those who wanted to jump straight down in front of a train' (Markham). However, its worst local tragedy came on 5 June 1847: the pointsman on duty at Blue Bridge, Bernard Fossey, was responsible for an horrific accident at Wolverton. He had apparently switched the London mail train into a goods siding where it crashed into some coal wagons, killing seven people and injuring many more.

Blue Bridge, looking east towards Bradville, 1997 (MH). In happier and more parochial times, two wells were sunk by the LNW Railway company just south of Blue Bridge and east of the railway line, for the supply of water to the residents of Wolverton and New Bradwell — their employees. It was pumped to two tanks at the top of Wolverton and gravity-fed to both communities.

Aerial shot of Blue Bridge (bottom left) and Wolverton Works, 1974 (CNT). The history of the Blue Bridge area goes back farther than its 19th-century railway constructions, however. Close to the old LNWR pumping station (left) just north of the Bancroft Villa excavations, a Roman burial mound was unearthed in 1981. It was discovered when preparations were being made by contractors for a new foul sewer for the Loughton Valley.

A brooch, probably Roman, found in the Blue Bridge area, c. 1980 (CNT). There was great excitement when the mound was revealed to be the mausoleum of a family 'of considerable wealth and importance' (Mynard). There was some poignancy, too, in the bodies found in the eight graves: three of them were men aged 30–50 years, one was a pregnant woman aged 18–24 years, and there were four children under 4 years of age. One of the individuals was 5 ft 2½ in, had had abcesses in his mouth, and had suffered from osteo-arthritis from an early age. Then, as now, riches did not always provide a trouble-free life!

The 1989 combined population estimate of Bancroft and Blue Bridge was 1,890.

CHAPTER FOUR

BRADVILLE

Aerial view of the Bradville estate, looking north, 1970 (CNT). The original 1930s housing estate is shown before any new city development. The canal crosses the centre, with the Bradwell Lake beyond. The unsevered Bradwell Road emerges bottom centre from Old Bradwell Village, where it had been Loughton Road.

The Bradville estate originally derived its name from Bournville, the much-acclaimed garden suburb on the Cadbury estate in Birmingham, when Wolverton Urban District Council (WUDC) began new housing development along the Bradwell Road in the 1930s.

Much of the land used to be owned by Farmer Robert Wylie – who represented New Bradwell on the then new Bucks County Council in 1889. 'Us kids didn't like him at all. If he caught kids blackberrying, bird-nesting or bird-hopping, he came after you on his horse. If he caught you and was in a bad mood, he'd make you tip your blackberries out on the floor and stamp on them.' When he died, however, he left instructions in his will that the old people of New Bradwell should receive a pension of a hundredweight of coal and two loaves (Hawtin Mundy).

It was estimated in 1927 that £500 would buy a house with 'a good-sized living-room, scullery, bathroom and three bedrooms'. In 1972 new city housing was developed on the estate by the Milton Keynes Development Corporation. The artist Eugene Fisk commented: 'Bradville has a uniform style, softened throughout by spacious undulations of grassed areas.'

Milton Keynes' first solar house was built at Bradville in 1975, and in 1976 employment was established on the estate. Its estimated population in 1989 was 3,760.

Bucks county councillors visiting the Kingsfold showhouse with leaders of Milton Keynes Development Corporation, August 1974 (CNT). Left to right: John Stevenson, BCC Chief Executive Officer; John Routley, Chairman of BCC Policy and Resources Committee; Lord Campbell, MKDC Chairman; James Ireland, BCC Chairman; Fred Lloyd Roche, MKDC General Manager.

The Bradville solar house – the city's first – in Harrowden, *c.* 1975 (CDC/CNT).

Aerial view of Kingsfold (right) and Crispin (left) in modern Bradville, *c.* 1975 (CDC/CNT). Pepper Hill First School is lower left, with the old Vicarage for New Bradwell's St James's Church bottom right.

The Limes, Bradwell Road, Bradville, 1997 (MH). The Limes, near Ashwood, bears the initials of the landowner, Robert Wylie, and the date 1871. He held office as a parish councillor non-stop for 33 years, having started in public life 20 years before that. He was chairman of many local organisations including the School Board, the Conservative Association, the Good Samaritans, the Allotment Holders and, of course, the Parish Council.

The Memorial at New Bradwell, c. 1930 (CDC/Kitchener). In 1917 – a full 20 months before the First World War finally ended – Councillor Wylie offered to fund a monument to those who had died (and were still to die). He envisaged it as 11 ft high in white Sicilian marble, surmounted by the figure of a soldier in field uniform. It was to be in the New Cemetery at the top of the hill (now by the V8/V7 roundabout), 'away from the crowd and away from the smoke . . .'. It would have space for 50 to 70 inscriptions – a chilling thought for those men who were still serving. It would be, the Parish Council averred, 'a memorial free from any criticism or bias from any body or sect. There is nothing in it that will give any offence . . .'. Unfortunately, the statue of the soldier was thought by some to be far too small and was subsequently removed, to great local consternation. It has since been put back, though it looks a little battered.

Mill Cottage being restored in August 1974. The Limes is in the background (CNT). After Robert's death, the house was home to John Alexander Wylie for much of the first half of this century. In December 1927, the wedding reception for his sister, Miss Mary Wylie, was held at the house. On her marriage to Mr Harry Pateman of Turvey, she wore Russian sables and received presents of cut glass and silver from many local organisations – such as the Stantonbury Mothers' Meeting of which she had been president for 18 years.

Her life of comparative luxury was in stark contrast to that of a real 'Stantonbury mother'. Just a week previously at the Newport Pagnell petty sessions, a bigamously married wife from New Bradwell tried to obtain over £16 in arrears from the father of her two children, aged 6 and 4. The court ruled against her: the man, it was felt, had served his sentence for bigamy, was ill and out of work; she, however, had a part-time insurance job bringing in 22s a week. The arrears were cancelled and the weekly maintenance order was reduced from 6 to 4s per child.

The old Vicarage, Bradwell Road, Bradville, 1997 (MH). In Ashwood, the old Vicarage of New Bradwell – some distance from its Church of St James – was designed by G.E. Street, designer of the law courts in the Strand in London. It originally stood in almost 2 acres of land. Reg Mynard remembered 'imposing iron gates at the North entrance, a sweeping drive to the stables. Huge trees screened it . . . and there was a system of bells to every room to summon the servants.' Sidney Teagle remembered the Vicarage being 'cold and bare'. Charles Sambrook remembered how, during the war, the air raid wardens had a little hut on Father Guest's tennis courts; their wives made out the duty rosters, and also did first aid and nursing there.

An early view of Bradwell Windmill and Mill Cottage, *c.* 1900 (WDAS). Mill Lane is named after an important local landmark, the listed 19th-century Bradwell Windmill, built just before the Industrial Revolution. Shortly after the Cosgrove–Buckingham canal branch line opened in 1801, Samuel Holman hoped to capitalise on the new commercial prospects it offered. He bought an acre of land known as the Yawles from Henry Wilmin, so as to erect a 'smock mill' – where just the cap and sails turn to meet the wind, not the whole body. A tower windmill was eventually built from local stone in 1815 at a cost of £500. It had blades and sailcloths 52 ft in diameter.

The windmill and cottage, 1997 (MH). The Bradwell Mill had a working life of only about 50 years. Robert Adams of Bradwell Abbey bought it in 1857, but by 1864, after John Abbott had bought it for £422 10s, the sails had revolved commercially for the last time. By 1876 the efficiency of the railway network sealed the fate of such small mills forever.

An aerial view of the windmill in 1974 during reconstruction, with Goodman's Yard (top) (CNT). The mill was recognised in 1949 by WUDC as an important pre-industrial monument and narrowly escaped demolition to be partially restored. In 1967 a tremendous gale blew one of the sails off; the other was hastily dismantled as a precaution. However, MKDC bought it and brought it back to full working order in 1969.

The old windmill with the 'Nobby' train passing by, *c.* 1910 (WDAS). Reg Mynard's memories of the mill include 'climbing up through wooden floors on creaking, dusty, half-rotten steps right to the cap. It was possible to see for miles around . . .'. Between the windmill and the canal is the line of the former Wolverton–Newport Pagnell 'Nobby' railway, now a cycle redway. The listed Mill Cottage is also late 18th century.

The Bradville estate: Stanton Avenue leading to Althorpe Crescent, 1930s (CDC/Kitchener). These were the original Bradville houses built by WUDC in the 1930s. Residents first moved in when the road was still muddied from recent completion. Everything in those days was delivered to the door: 'Milk was measured out, the Co-op breadman came, Herrington came from Loughton with coal, the butcher's boy delivered . . . we had a very good going on, till the War started' (Charles Sambrook).

The same view, 1997 (MH). Stanton Avenue derives its name from the ancient village deserted since the 16th century; and Althorpe Crescent from Earl Spencer's ancestral home in Northamptonshire – now almost a shrine to the late Diana, Princess of Wales.

Bradwell Road at the junction with Abbey Way, *c.* 1930 (BCC/Kitchener). Residents on the Bradville estate had a quaint water supply in the early days of the '30s: a pump had been installed for them beneath the railway bridge (now going over the redway) at Bradwell station. However, whenever a train filled up with water there, the pump automatically shut off! This was not popular on washdays. Eventually, engine drivers were ordered to fill up at Wolverton.

The same junction, 1997 (MH). Bradvue Crescent, Bridle Close and Abbotts Close lead off from Abbey Way. A terrible fire gutted one of the post-war prefabs here in January 1947. The hapless mother had left her 14-month-old child strapped in a high chair while she went to get some shopping. When she returned, her house was an inferno, and her child burnt beyond recognition. The cause of the fire was never established, but the community gave the family much support, raising over £100 in donations – about 20 weeks' pay in those days.

Aerial view of Bradville, 29 July 1977 (CNT). The Bradville advanced factory units are in the foreground, with the new Bradville housing above and Stantonbury Campus lower right. The Grand Union Canal runs across the top third of the picture with New Bradwell beyond that.

Some of the place names chosen by MKDC for the modern Bradville estate have strong connections with the history and traditions of the old Bradwell parish: Thomas Mercer, for example, was recorded in 1783 as the owner of the Bradwell Manor estate; Sir William Vaux of Vauxhall was Lord of the Manor of Stantonbury in the 15th century. A leader of the Lancastrians in the Wars of the Roses, he was killed in the battle of Tewkesbury in 1471. It was his successor, Sir Nicholas Vaux, a trusted favourite and counsellor of Henry VIII, who caused the death of Stantonbury village. In about 1510, he converted his 36 acres of land at Stanton Low to sheep-raising; 40 people were put out of work and deprived of their homes. By 1563, only three households remained. It took just a little more time before Stantonbury was populated only by hundreds of sheep. Indeed by 1876, 'Staunton' ceased to appear on maps of the area; it had been recorded until then by cartographers since the first Buckinghamshire map of 1574; a barry was the name of a medieval farming practice where a field was divided horizontally into equal parts by bars of two colours alternating; it was also the name of one of the owners of the Bradwell Abbey estate, Peter Barry, in the 13th century; Miles Crispin, along with Walter Giffard, became an owner of Bradwell Manor after the Norman Conquest.

Aerial view of Harrowden with its solar house, 8 June 1979 (CNT). The Baron of Harrowden in Northamptonshire was Sir Nicholas Vaux, the destroyer of Stantonbury village. After he bought a pardon in 1523, he was created baron. Thomas Vaux, his son, was painted by the famous Holbein; the original drawing is in the Royal Collection at Windsor.

The Stanton Low grazing fields, 1997 (MH). Stanton County Middle School is on the site of Stanton High, owned by Farmer Wylie. His cattle used to be driven from Wolverton station – the car park there was a cattle landing – to Stanton High to feed there for a while. Then they were driven about a mile due north, crossing both railway and canal (left of picture) to reach their meadow pastures at Stanton Low. The beef farm was famous even in London's Smithfield Market where signs would advertise 'Prime Stanton Low Beef'.

Aerial view of the Bradville estate, 26 May 1965 (Aerofilms). This pre-Milton Keynes picture shows the Bradwell Road running from bottom right to left centre, where it crosses the old railway line which stretches towards Great Linford, top right; Newport Road runs along the top of the picture, crossing the Grand Union Canal, top centre left; in between, around and beyond, undisturbed farmland.

CHAPTER FIVE

NEW BRADWELL

Spencer Street, New Bradwell, c. 1970 (CDC/CNT). The street used to run the full length of the High Street before Wolverton Urban District Council began whole-scale demolition of all its 19th-century railway cottages during the period 1965–75.

ew Bradwell was originally known by residents as Stantonbury – and named as such on local
buses – until well into the 1930s. In 1851, its population was 381. By 1861, there were 1,658
inhabitants, with 46 local businesses operating. By 1871, the population had grown to 2,409; to
2,906 in 1891; and by 1900, 3,512 people lived there with 79 local trades. In 1919, it severed its parish
connection with Old Bradwell and became a ward of the newly formed Wolverton Urban District
Council. The estimated population in 1989 was 2,540.

At the beginning of the 19th century, a canal wharf was established at what would become New
Bradwell for the newly constructed Grand Junction Canal (later Grand Union). When the Railway Works
expanded in the 1850s, the London and North Western Railway company bought 15 acres of arable land
between the canal and the turnpike road, and 4 acres of meadow adjoining Bradwell Brook, at a cost of
£150 an acre. Between 1854 and 1860, the company built a self-sufficient community for its employees
and their families. In the first phase, there were over 200 houses with shops, a church, a school and even a
purpose-built pub, The Forester's Arms, run first by Thomas Copson, then George Chaplin (1876),
Edward Huckle (1887) and Arthur Toogood (1899). The new estate was a 'sister colony' for Wolverton,
according to the *Illustrated London News* in June 1856: 'The cottages are remarkably neat in appearance and
are built in the most substantial manner with regard to every comfort and convenience of the residents.'

The foundation stone-laying ceremony was performed by 'the Marquis of Chandos and his noble lady. . . .
The company afterwards repaired to a spacious marquee erected in an adjoining field and partook of
refreshments. The workmen of the company and their families were provided with a substantial meal
under the same roof.'

However, there were early indications that conditions would be crowded: in 1865, a random count of
a third of the houses revealed that 65 cottages had 327 rooms for 523 occupants – an average household of
8 people. Further building in 1901 made Wolverton/New Bradwell the second largest town in the county
with a combined population total of 9,200. Only High Wycombe was larger; but it took time for 20th-
century conveniences to arrive. In 1927, 338 households were still dependent on wells for water, and gas
mains for all were not due to arrive for another 18 months; new electric light poles had just been installed
– although even these had problems: the local paper reported how a 'young lady had run into one pole
and as a result of the collision, it was two or three weeks before she thoroughly recovered . . .'.

In 1965, when it cost around £1,500 to buy a terraced house, or £3,425 for a detached house, the
WUDC declared the ageing and unmodernised railway cottages as a clearance area and, despite their
Grade III listing, began to demolish them. By 1975, all but two terraces in Spencer Street had disappeared
when a public enquiry upheld their conservation; MKDC purchased and improved them.

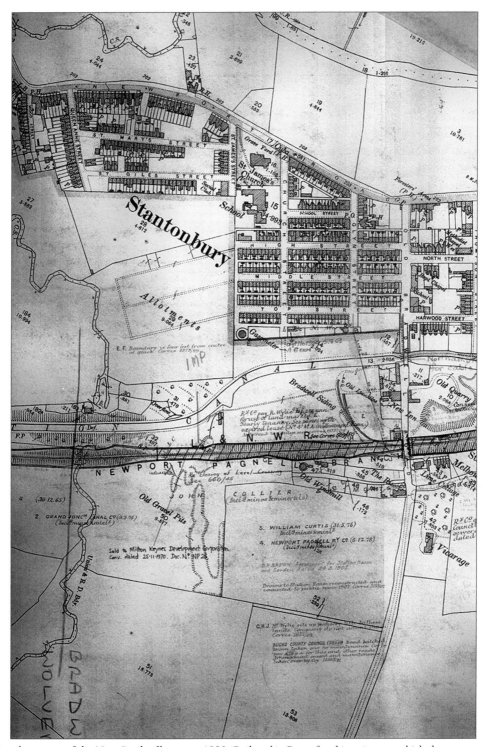

A railway map of the New Bradwell area, *c.* 1890 (Railtrack). Part of an historic map which shows around 100 years of property transactions from 1876 ('William Curtis', right) to 1970 ('Sold to Milton Keynes Development Corporation', left).

An early picture of Stantonbury Road, Wolverton – with Stonebridgehouse Farm on the right – later known as Newport Road, New Bradwell (WDAS). In 1819, the traveller John Hassell described the road as 'a very pleasant road with an abundance of lofty trees'. Forty years later, many of them had to be felled for purpose-built homes for the community of railway workers.

View to New Bradwell Clock Tower at the 'Corner Pin' from Wolverton Station Hill, *c.* 1970 (CNT).

The County Arms and Corner Pin, *c.* 1920 (WDAS). The County Arms Hotel, built in 1854, is on the bend of the original Newport Road near where the clock tower stands. Its large assembly room was used by auctioneers, travelling salesmen and concert parties. It also had a covered bowling alley, known as 'Pin Alley' – possibly the origin of the name of the bend in the road known to locals as the 'Corner Pin'. At the turn of the century, annual smoking concerts were held at the pub. By the 1930s, dances were held there every week – sometimes two or three times. Early landlords included St John Allen (1876), Harriet Allen (1887), and John Smith (1899).

The same view, 1997 (MH). Here, 16 bronze fragments of tools and weapons from the prehistoric Middle Bronze Age (*c.* 1500 BC) were discovered in 1879. There were '9 socketed celts (chisels), 3 broken celts, 1 palstave (shaped chisel head), 2 spearheads and a leaf-shaped sword broken into 4 pieces' in a 'deep cist, filled with black earth and about 18 inches deep' (*British Archaeological Report*, no. 34, 1977). Aerial photographs also show ring ditches, possibly Bronze Age burial mounds, suggesting extensive settlement along the Ouse valley.

Corner Pin in the snow, *c.* 1910 (WDAS). The shop (left) was kept by Syd Mynard until 1914, then became Green's antique shop. Almost directly north of the County Arms (right), on the S-bend of the river, is the site of the bathing place created for residents in about 1915. 'The shallow end was 5 yards in diameter . . . it had a wooden catwalk, a spring board and access steps. The changing room was an old railway carriage' (Reg Mynard). In 1937, R. Bellchambers, then the press secretary of the New Bradwell League of Youth, wrote to the local paper to complain of the 'disgrace' of the 'dressing arrangements: there are two enclosures which I refrain from calling sheds . . . I should imagine they formed part of Stephenson's first railway train!'

The old bathing place on the River Ouse, July 1997 (MH). The bathing place caused a few more upsets in its lifetime: in 1917, an ongoing feud between Councillors Puryer and Wilson spilled over during a seemingly innocuous debate about tree-planting there. One offended the other who declared, 'It's a jolly rotten shame to make the remark he did!' The offender 'absolutely refused to withdraw it!' As a result, the tree-planting was deferred until, three months later, the offender resigned. The bathing place was closed and dismantled in the 1940s because the water, from storm-water drains and from under the Carriage Works, was deemed to be too polluted. There was some consternation in council meetings when children were reported using the canal instead.

Surveying across Corner Pin for a straighter Newport Road, 1937 (BCC). The Corner Pin might also be so named because of the sharpness of the bend. A 1904 census of traffic revealed how busy it was: from 5 a.m. to 10 p.m. on a June day, 6,982 pedestrians were counted along with 332 horse-drawn vehicles, 425 bicycles and motors, 361 'perambulators and handcarts', 17 horses, 2 donkeys, 1 flock of sheep, 1 steam-threshing outfit and 3 monkeys! It was calculated that if there could be a straighter path, cutting the route by 205 yards, it would make the difference of 200 miles a year 'to any person living in Stantonbury (New Bradwell) and going home for meals'.

The straighter Newport Road, 60 years later, in 1997 (MH). In 1937, improvements to the A422 indeed added a straight run from the foot of Wolverton Station Hill, although not without a few sparks flying at council meetings. Councillor Jeffs accused Councillor Brown of unreasonable delay: 'You have not put as much effort into this road as you did in the Haversham Road improvements!'

Floods at Corner Pin, 1968 (WDAS). Corner Pin was known as the poorest part of New Bradwell, possibly because it was so vulnerable to floods, not only from the River Ouse, but also from the Bradwell Brook. In March 1937, the *Express* reported: 'The Bradwell Brook was much swollen and on Friday evening 23 sheep were found to have been drowned at Stacey Hill Farm.' Flooding was particularly bad in 1939 when the river rose to 11 ft above its normal level.

Floods at Haversham Road Bridge, just north of New Bradwell, 18 October 1939 (LAP). The pressure of the water was so great that it simply lifted the bridge up.

Floods at Corner Pin in 1939 (the white mark top left is on the original photograph!) (BCC). The building on the left used to be the Liberal Hall where weekly concerts – called 'A Pleasant Sunday Afternoon' – used to be held. Later, as now, it housed 'Telfer's Builders'. In more temperate times than the floods shown in the picture, the brook was home to 'huge shoals of minnows and fry, of roach and bream', congregating where the brook joined the Ouse (Reg Mynard).

The same site in 1997 (MH). The boys of Wolverton and Bradwell congregated there too. 'There was great rivalry in those days – we would meet at the 'Seven Sisters', seven poplar trees. That's where we had a mud battle, at the Brook there', recalled Hawtin Mundy. He was also summonsed, along with five of his friends, for 'playing football to the detriment of traffic on the public highway'. They had to appear at Newport Court and were each fined 6s – for kicking a tennis ball about on the Newport Road!

A flower wagon at the Hospital Fête, *c.* 1910 (LAP). The Corner Pin was also the venue for the annual
Stantonbury Whitsun Fête, to raise money for Northampton Hospital. The parade would start at the west
end with dozens of horse-drawn floats. Hundreds of crêpe paper flowers decorated the streets, and songs
and dances were performed.

Nellie Abbey (née Smith), *c.* 1910 (LAP). Nellie Smith, whose father ('Piccolo' Smith) was a founder
member of the Bradwell Band, was well known for her energetic preparations for the fête. Iris Davies
remembered how 'she was always in trouble at work in the Sewing Room (Wolverton Works) because she
was always rehearsing her singing and bits and bobs'.

The Whit Monday 'Coon Concert', 27 May 1912 (LAP). Nellie is in the front row, second from right. 'She played the banjo – had a little band called the "Mandolin Band" and they played for weddings and dances' (Iris Davies). Later, as Mrs Nellie Abbey, she was a core organiser for fête activities; every year, the local newspaper would commend her efforts: 'Carnival Melody was presented by the Stantonbury Girls' Club under the experienced and able direction of Mrs. Abbey . . .' (Wolverton Express, June 1927).

Effie Grant, Nellie's friend, c. 1912 (LAP).

Nellie (middle row left) as Little Bo Peep and Effie (front row centre, sitting) as a clown, ready for the Fancy Dress Parade, *c.* 1910 (LAP).

The 'Britannia' wagon for the Whitsun Fête, *c.* 1913 (LAP). Nellie and Effie stand at the front on either side of the wagon.

Nellie holding the reins of the 'Shamrock Car', *c.* 1920 (LAP).

Miss Stokes of St Giles Street, Miss Green, Miss Trodd and Mrs Brooks are all said to feature in this fête photograph, *c.* 1910 (MKM).

Lining up by the 'Rec' in Newport Road, *c.* 1912 (MKM). Large crowds would watch the walking race along the Newport Road, from Newport Pagnell police station to the specially marked out 'Rec' – the Bradwell recreation ground opposite the Corner Pin. There were children's races and the women's egg-and-spoon race; there were pillow fights on a pole and 'holding the greased pig' while singing a song; and there was 'tilting the bucket' – men driving boys in wheelbarrows at speed aiming at a bucket full of water on a pole; the drivers invariably got soaked!

The main speaker at the 'Rec' Fête is Mr J. Purves, Wolverton Works Superintendent and the Watford–Rugby Main Line Manager. Councillor Albert Brown is to his right, *c.* 1935 (MKM). Once, the men's 100-yard race caused much dispute: the winner, named Boone, was said to have broken the world record, inside 10 seconds, but Hawtin Mundy retorted: 'Their 100 yards was 90 yards, and on top of that, I think they timed him with a grandfather clock!' The last fête was held in 1941.

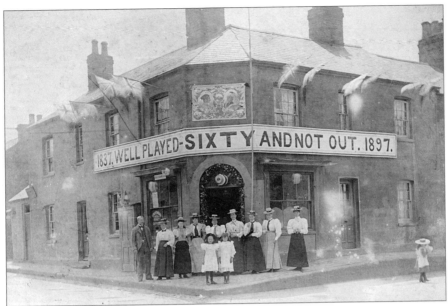

The Cuba Hotel, on the corner with Church Street, seen here in the year of Victoria's Diamond Jubilee, 1897 (MKM). The Cuba Hotel opened in 1864 with William Harding as landlord. Lily Stonton used to live there as one of 14 children: her father, Thomas Giltrow, was landlord for 45 years; 6 brothers fought in the First World War and 3 sisters were on war work. She recalled Dr Miles being so impressed with her putting a boy's broken leg in a splint that he wanted her to become a nurse, but her father needed her in the pub. Later, in 1947, landlady Irene Trunder sued one of her customers, Reginald Jackson of St Giles Street, for assault. She had refused to marry him; they had fought. They continued arguing in court, so the magistrate interrupted the proceedings which clearly bored him and dismissed the case.

The Cuba pub, 1997 (MH). Opposite the Cuba was 'Giltrow's field'. Sometimes, Romany caravans would park there with their traditional scrap-iron business, but the field often flooded. It would also be the venue for a 'Travelling Gaff' or 'Penny Gaff', where plays were put on in a tent. Lily Stonton remembered seeing *Uncle Tom's Cabin* and *Murder in the Red Barn*. 'Inside was a stage and forms to sit on. In front of the stage was two braziers to keep the place warm in the cold weather. The kids used to put potatoes on them – alright until someone put a bloater on them and stank the place out!' (Hawtin Mundy).

Harry Lines's barber's shop, Newport Road, *c.* 1900 (MKM). This shop was next to the Cuba. Once, when the circus came to town and set up in Giltrow's field (1 July 1900), Harry became famous for going into the lion tamer's cage; he was presented with a certificate recording how he 'successfully performed the feat of Shaving the Keeper while in the den'. On Harry's death in 1940, his son Fred continued the business until he too died, in 1947.

The same site in 1997 (MH).

Newport Road was the source of many local stories reported by the *Wolverton Express*. At the Forester's Arms in November 1891, an impromptu inquest was held on the same day as the discovery in the River Ouse of the body of 48-year-old Samuel Teagle. He had been missing for three weeks. He had lost his job at the works 'for excessive loss of time' and had become very depressed, his wife Rebecca testified. As his father had committed suicide before him, the coroner promptly recorded a similar verdict. No mention is made of any autopsy!

A year later, the death of Edward Huckle was announced – landlord of the pub for 14 years. At his funeral on 31 October 'nearly all the leading tradesmen of the place were present, most of whom had the blinds of their houses drawn at the hour of the funeral in token of their sincere respect and sorrow'.

Albert Brown, a well-known union activist of the 1926 General Strike, lived in Newport Road. The railway workers at New Bradwell – 'Little Moscow' – were considered to be far more militant than in Wolverton. However, after the strike, Albert Brown left the shop-floor for the offices, and later became a leading public figure as a councillor and JP. For some, this represented a betrayal of the workers; for others, he was a much respected member of the community. In August 1937, the *Express* reported a dramatic rescue when Mr Brown and his wife tried to get into a boat moored at the bottom of their garden. They both fell in and were saved from drowning only by a fisherman visiting from London.

A barge in the ice of the Grand Union Canal near New Bradwell (MKM). Another notable resident was Polly the Parrot, owned by a retired baker, Scotty Edwards, whose house backed on to the canal. Hawtin Mundy remembered how, as kids, they taught her to say 'Gee up!' and 'Whoa!' to the boat horses as they passed her on her tree perch. 'The boatees used to go as mad as hell. One man threatened, "I'll get off at the bridge – I'll wring that bloody parrot's neck!" Well, one cold night, Scotty forgot to fetch Polly in and she died. The legend after that was that when the horses came along the canal and found Polly was dead, they said the horses used to stop and bow their heads!'

Newport Road at the Bradwell Road junction, looking east, *c.* 1930 (CDC/Kitchener). The Labour Hall (left) in Newport Road used to be a shop owned by Mr J.E. Nutt, farrier, blacksmith and wheelwright. Children went to him for toy iron hoops which cost a penny. Reg Mynard remembers it as a small engineering firm. Nearby were river meadows where the horses were put out to pasture. During 1957, the hall played host to the famous Rockets, a local rock 'n' roll band, led by Terry Carroll. Admission was 2*s* 6*d*.

Newport Road, looking east, 1997 (MH).

Newport Road at the Glyn Street junction, looking west, *c.* 1920 (BCC). The imposing building to the right of the picture, built in 1919, used to be a Working Men's Club. It is now a dance school.

Newport Road, looking west, 1997 (MH). In April 1966, during her visit to the area, the Queen travelled along the Newport Road, although New Bradwell residents caught only the merest glimpse of her as the royal car drove round the Corner Pin. Nevertheless, Brownies and Cubs had been hand-picked to salute her as she glided past at 5 m.p.h.

Queen Anne Street, *c.* 1930 (CDC/Kitchener). Queen Anne Street has been witness to some singular and diverse events in the town: it saw the inauguration of New Bradwell's first Working Men's Club on 1 August 1893 before it moved to neighbouring St Giles Street. In November 1917, a resident of the street, Mrs Keightley, suffered a tragic double loss: her 63-year-old father, Henry West, came to give her the news about the death in the war of her brother; but he was himself so shocked by the news that he collapsed and died in front of her of a heart attack.

Queen Anne Street, 1997 (MH). Stantons the Bakers used to be at the junction with the Newport Road. Children would stand by the gratings to warm their hands and enjoy the delicious smells. Another trader in the street, Frank Gostelow, received a boost in 1937: the Parish Council ordered 800 Coronation cups and saucers from him which they planned to present to all the schoolchildren of the town. The celebrations would also include fancy dress parades, children's teas, sports, a bonfire and a torchlight procession.

Corner Pin Fête, *c.* 1905 (WDAS). Queen Anne Street gave access to the field where all this would take place – now occupied by the Clock Tower Gardens. It was also the site of an annual cycle parade, attended by the many cycle clubs which had developed since the turn of the century. Travelling fairs and circuses would set up here too – Giles Thurston's famous fair organ giving recitals of sacred music and John Sanger's circus steam engines using the Bradwell Brook for water.

The Clock Tower Gardens, 1997 (MH). The New Bradwell Silver Band played at the bandstand, opened in 1903. A bandsman recalls how they used to time the beat of the music according to the thickness of the grass – to enable people to dance! However, even in 1903, townsfolk despaired of how some young people behaved in this new facility. Councillor Puryer complained that the 'cheek of some of the lads . . . was abominable. One lad had a carpet fixed to two trees and was swinging on this and when told to take it down refused to do so.' He was outraged at their 'playing on the steps of the bandstand, climbing up the sides and destroying fences!'

May Day Fête at the 'Rec', *c.* 1910 (MKM). There was a fair at the 'Rec' every August. Tom Blunt could remember buying 'squibs' for a halfpenny: these were like toothpaste tubes, only larger and made of lead. 'You filled them with water, walked round the fair, followed the girls and squibbed water down their necks!' He also watched 'spit rock' being made: 'They mixed treacle and sugar in a bowl, drew it out as it stiffened, spat on their hands and stretched it out. They had a big hook on the side of the caravans, and drew it out more on that.'

Corner Pin Jubilee Party at the 'Rec', 1935 (MKM). Hawtin Mundy also remembered the leisure pursuits of the 'aristocrats', such as the sons and daughters of publicans and shopkeepers: 'They were all top-notchers. We kids used to collect the "keck" which grew in the hedgerows, about 2–3 feet high. The stems were hollow, so you'd cut a piece off, get hips and haws and lean over the hedge and blow through the pipes at them as they played tennis!'

Caledonian Road in the snow, 1916 (WDAS). The Sunday School here was called the 'Tin Hut' (Hawtin Mundy). Between Caledonian Road and the railway line were the sewage works and the rubbish tip – the cause of much heated debate in the '30s. In August 1937, a frustrated Councillor Jeffs declared, 'They must collect dead cats and dead dogs. . . . When people in the vicinity get to bed at nights, the smell from the burning is enough to poison one. It's reports, reports, reports – when are they going to get on with the job and get something done?'

Caledonian Road, *c.* 1930 (CDC/Kitchener).

Caledonian Road, 1997 (MH).

The opening ceremony for the Clock Tower
Gardens, c. 1955 (MKM). Other Corner Pin
roads include Wallace Street, just off
Caledonian Road, which also had problems
with flooding: in October 1939, along with
neighbouring streets, it was under several
feet of water – the 'worst floods ever'. A
happier event was celebrated on 7 September
1940 when Mrs Hannah Matthews, who
lived in this street with her daughter, became
one of the town's oldest-ever residents – at
101. Wood Street was where the depot for
'Mutual Coal' was – a friendly society paying
dividends to those who paid money into it. It
has since been converted into a flat.

St Marys Street, *c.* 1930 (CDC/Kitchener). Along with King Edward Street and St Giles Street, St Marys was open land until around 1890, when more houses were built to accommodate the swell of new workers. Frederick Church remembers paying 10*s* rent for his house in the 1930s and later buying it for £110.

St Marys Street, 1997 (MH).

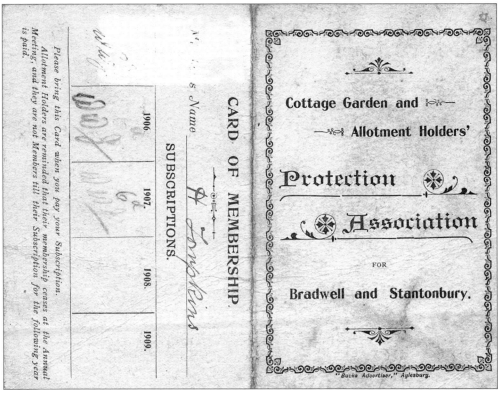

Cottage Garden and Allotment Holders' Protection Card, 1907 (MKM). The association's 'protective' function, in an age without state welfare or support, was made all too clear in a sad case reported in the local paper in 1927: A young man, aged 20, had been seen stealing from the allotments by Obadiah

Dowdy of Wallace Street and Ellen Miller of Bridge Street. After a chase, he was found hiding in the lavatory of one of the houses in St Marys Street. His grandparents and father (residents of the street) would have nothing to do with him. He had spent his youth in the Reformatory; then he had been sent to Canada, deported back to England, sent to Borstal, and finally to Wormwood Scrubs prison.

On release, he was ordered to go to the Newport Pagnell Workhouse, but 'he refused to stop there and became abusive'. He had taken 'a handful and a half of gooseberries', because, he said, he had 'had no food for two days and wanted something to keep himself alive'. He was sent to prison for seven days and then ordered back to Borstal.

Tarry's Butcher's Shop of St Marys Street, 1975 (CNT). The shop closed in 1980 and is now a private residence, no. 27.

St Marys Street corner shop, *c.* 1970 (CNT). This shop, on the corner with Queen Ann Street, was at one time used by Mr Beech on behalf of the Parish Council for collecting rents. It was also used as a temporary surgery when Dr Love's residence was damaged by the 1940 bombing raid.

St Marys Street old corner shop, 1997 (MH). The dwelling to the right of the old shop used to be Knight's the Cobblers.

The junction of St Giles Street with St James Street, *c.* 1975 (CNT). Here New Bradwell's first Working Men's Club had the foundation date of 1894 inscribed in the stone. Its signboard is top right of the picture.

The same junction in 1997 (MH). Nine years before the advent of the Working Men's Club, in 1885, Mr and Mrs J. Jones were the first couple to be married at St James's Church at a Sunday morning service, performed by its first vicar, Revd Mr Cotter. They had moved into 14 St Giles Street when it was new, and were still resident there in 1937, 42 years later.

St Giles Street, *c.* 1930 (CDC/Kitchener).

St Giles Street, 1997 (MH).

The St Giles 'Stantonbury Working Men's Club', *c.* 1905 (MKM). This picture postcard was sent to Miss Nellie Claridge of 19 Spencer Street on 25 September 1906.

King Edward Street, *c.* 1930 (CDC/Kitchener). New Bradwell was known as Little Moscow during the 1926 General Strike, with King Edward Street as 'the most Bolshie street in Bradwell'! Eric Bellchambers remembers how 'blacklegs' had to be escorted to the works and home again – 'about 40 police and these miserable little six men in the middle of them' – while the strikers sang 'See the conquering heroes come!' Frances Welch's mother was on the receiving end of such ill-feeling: 'Although she was bedridden, she went to the door one night and said to the crowd, "Why do you do this? We haven't done you any harm. I'll ask God to forgive you all tonight." And a man struck her across the face with an umbrella. He went to prison!'

King Edward Street Jubilee celebrations, 1935 (MKM). In 1937, like at the Jubilee of 1935, all was smiles and jubilation when one of the activists of the General Strike, now Councillor Albert Brown, presented the street with the shield for the best Coronation street-decoration: 'a real work of art', he said. Residents had worked on their secret design from 4 a.m. until 9 a.m. on Coronation Day. Then the festivities began – and continued for five days! 'Thousands of people and hundreds of cars passed down the street during the day. . . . Dancing and games were indulged in the street in the evening to music supplied by Mr. Baldwin and his fellow bandsmen . . . until a late hour' (*Express*).

King Edward Street, 1997 (MH). In 1982 another King Edward Street resident recalled a more subdued royal event – the day Queen Victoria died, in 1901: 'We weren't allowed to do anything – not allowed to play in the streets, only walk gently around' (Mr Baldwin).

Hawtin Mundy in 1985 (LAP). King Edward Street's best-known resident, Hawtin Mundy's marvellous memories were recorded by Living Archive (LAP) and have spawned a musical documentary play, *Days of Pride*; local and national radio programmes; an award-winning one-man show at the Edinburgh Festival, performed by local actor Brad Bradstock who lives in neighbouring Spencer Street; and two books – *'I'll tell you what happened'* and *'No heroes, no cowards'* (both published by LAP). Before moving to King Edward Street, Hawtin had lived in North Street and Thompson Street.

Sending off recruits from Wolverton station, 1914 (LAP). Hawtin's descriptions of his First World War experiences are particularly poignant: 'I don't believe there was such a thing as heroes or cowards during that war. I was in it from the first week to the finish, that included trench warfare, battle of the Somme, battle of Arras, 20 months as prisoner of war and collected three lots of wounds on the way. We were not really soldiers at all, we were just civilians with guns in our hands, mainly young chaps.'

The 'War to end all wars' ended much more in the lives of ordinary families ensnared in it. Mr and Mrs Hollis, who were living at 14 Bounty Street in 1917, learned in March that their 20-year-old son had been killed in the war. His captain seemed to be struggling to give them comfort when he described the manner of his death: 'A shell burst through the roof and he was severely wounded. We got him to the dressing station in a few minutes and everything possible was done for him but he died very shortly afterwards. I don't think he suffered much pain, but as far as I can tell he was practically unconscious . . .'.

In the same year, a moving plea was made by a New Bradwell man not to be sent to the Front. As a conscientious objector with invalid parents he declared: 'It is wrong and barbarous to resort to force of arms to settle any dispute. . . . On the ground of humanity, tens of thousands of people have been put to death who had no quarrel with anyone, and on the Christian standpoint, we are told to love our enemies.' He was accused of 'being of two minds': while he objected to becoming a soldier, he continued to work for a company doing military work (Wolverton Works). His claim was dismissed.

Aerial view of Bounty Street, 1977 (CNT). Above the street is the New Bradwell County Combined School, with the old railway cottages of Spencer Street (left) undergoing renovation. Until well into the '20s, residents of Newport Road, St Marys, St Giles, King Edward, Queen Anne, Wallace and Wood Streets, and the Caledonian Road, would have to come to Bounty Street for buckets of fresh drinking water from the spring there, pumped from wells 20 ft deep. Town water was not available until the London Midland & Scottish Railway company laid new mains.

St James Street with the church grounds on the left, *c.* 1975 (CNT). St James's Church, part of the planned LNWR development, was designed by G.E. Street of London's Law Courts fame, built in 1858 at a cost of £4,430, and consecrated in 1860. James McConnell, the works' loco-superintendent, was a very supportive churchwarden – indeed, his son was the first to be baptised there. However, after a bitter dispute with the then chairman, Richard Moon, he resigned in 1862. The design had provided for a tower but when McConnell left, interest in the project waned and it was never built.

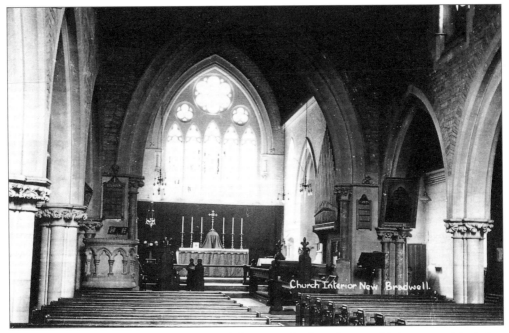

St James's Church interior (BCC). The stained glass is much admired: part of it is a memorial window installed in 1892 to celebrate the 33 years of service given by its first vicar, the Revd Mr Cotter. It has over its west door the Norman arch taken from the ancient ruin of St Peter's at Stanton Low.

Regular attenders at St James's Church, *c.* 1890 (MKM). Known faces are the Shouler brothers – Fred, back row second from right, and Walter, front row extreme left; the curate, Revd E. Marshall; and the Superintendent of the Sunday School, Mr Arkwright (bearded). Others not pinpointed are the Wylie brothers, local farmers; the Grant brothers, whose parents were grocers in the High Street; and the Lines brothers, sons of the famous barber, Harry Lines, in Newport Road.

Church Street had entrances both to the church and the school. It was part of the 15-acre development of houses, church, school, shops and public house built by LNWR between 1854 and 1861, and demolished by WUDC between 1965 and 1975. In the adjoining School Street was the Railway Tavern. In 1892, this was the impromptu venue for an inquest held on Lily Raffe, the infant daughter of Albert Raffe who had found her dead on the morning of 22 October. In the afternoon, the inquest ruled that as her parents testified that she had been ailing since her birth, seven weeks before, 'being afflicted with thrush and other diseases', she was deemed to have died of natural causes. The tavern lasted just 100 years, and was demolished in the 1950s.

Schoolchildren at the Church Street entrance to the school, 1908 (BCC). This well-known picture was on a postcard dated 26 September 1908 with a message to a Mrs Day in South Devon from her son. It reads: 'Dear Mother, Some mistake about my letter. Leslie *is* one of the assistants and these are some of the boys . . .'.

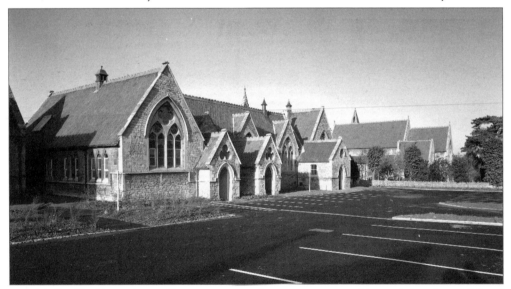

The old school buildings, designed by G.E. Street in about 1858, renovated by MKDC in about 1978 and now used as a community centre and workshops (CNT). The school was built next to St James's Church to be 'for the instruction of 100 girls and 100 boys and an infant school for the like number with dwellings for masters and/or mistresses' (*Illustrated London News*, 1856). One of the first headmasters, George Howitt, stayed for over 44 years, retiring in 1908. A pupil attending the Boys' School in 1908 described how the children were each charged a penny a week for lead pencil and slate and that the teacher would touch pupils with his pointer to see if they were awake! 'Scrubby' Dunbar and 'Lanky' Hall were among the teachers remembered there.

A class of New Bradwell schoolboys, 1910 (WDAS). The Infants' School log of 15 July 1911 describes how 'the little people plainly enjoy every minute of their school hours', but the headmistress, Miss Heacock, also criticised what she saw as outmoded premises: '(They) are exceedingly faulty. The two classrooms are particularly inconvenient and far too small. . . . This condition of things has existed for some years back but nothing in the way of remedying matters has, so far, been effected.'

New Bradwell schoolboys in class, c. 1920 (WDAS). In 1915, 45 children were excluded by the School Medical Officer on account of overcrowding; by 1916, 93 were excluded. November 1918 records the deaths of two infants from the influenza epidemic; and the cold winter of 1919, with indoor temperatures rarely exceeding freezing point, forced 'normal lessons to give place to a large proportion of physical exercise and all children were dressed in outdoor coats'.

BRADWELL & WOLVERTON
Good Samaritan Society.
Founded December 9th, 1872.

OFFICERS AND COMMITTEE, 1926.

President : C. Wylie, Esq.

Vice-Presidents :
Major C. L. Mason, M.C., R.E.
Capt. C. O. D. Anderson, H. E. Meacham, Esq.

Chairman : Mr. W. Heighton.

Vice-Chairman : Mr. J. Child.

Secretary :
Mr. A. E. Atterbury, 127, Church St., Wolverton.

Committee :
Messrs. G. Barden, A. Brazier, C. Bush,
A. Causer, H. Crane, B. Chaplin, F. Clarke,
A. Dinwiddy, S. W. Freeman, G. H. Hyde,
W. Kirk, W. Parkes, J. Parsons, Jun., W. Perkins,
F. Rose, W. Squire, R. Thompson, F. H. Tompkins,
H. Walton, J. Wells, S. H. Wheeldon, J.P.,
F. Wootton, and H. Wright.

Hon. Treasurer and Bankers :
Messrs. Barclay & Co. (Wolverton Branch).

Auditors :
Messrs. J. Rose and F. A. Thompson.

Headquarters :
Boys' School, Bounty Street, New Bradwell.

McCorquodale & Co. Ltd., Wolverton.

The Good Samaritan membership card, 1926 (MKM). The schools soon became an important meeting place for locals: in June 1892, the *Bucks Standard* reported some 'noisy proceedings' at a Conservative Association meeting there – the result of 'barracking from youths at the end of the room, interrupting . . . (being) painfully unpleasant with the singing of "Taraboom-de-ay" and whistling . . .'. Later, a 'happy gathering in the Girls' School' reported by the *Wolverton Express* in April 1927 was the 'annual tea and social of the New Bradwell Women Voters' League. . . . An excellent tea was provided to which about 200 sat down. A concert followed . . .'. Three weeks later, the New Bradwell Good Samaritan Society met for their AGM: Mr Chas Wylie, presiding, reported on 3,547 subscribers giving an average of 1*d* a week to fund such items as glasses, elastic stockings, trusses and surgical appliances for the poor and needy.

New Bradwell schoolboys, 1955 (WDAS). Ray Bellchambers is third from the left in the back row. The Spencer Street houses are behind. 'Speccy' Hyde is one trader many schoolchildren would have known: he used to sell sweets from a shop in School Street – which also sold coal!

New Bradwell schoolgirls, 1929 (WDAS). Front row, left to right: Mary Turner (later Bellchambers), Florrie Odell, Winifred Markham, Mabel Stephenson, Joyce Gardener – all from Old Bradwell Village. Mary remembers them each popping their potatoes in the gas oven for their dinners. There are some interesting log entries, too, for the girls' school during the Second World War: 46 evacuated children arrived in September 1939; an extra 48 a year later made the roll in each class over 50! Later, on 21 October 1940, the school was closed 'following extensive damage during an air raid yesterday evening', but by 4 November, it had reopened. In 1944, girls were being recruited by the WAEC to help with potato picking.

Back view of the old school buildings, *c.* 1970 (CNT). Lily Stonton remembered taking two evacuees into her home in School Street: 'There was a boy and a girl. Their parents never came to see them. I couldn't deal with the girl – she would scribble on the staircase as she went up. I got in touch with the authorities and she was moved.' She remembered an air raid too: 'I put the children in the cupboard and got in with them quick!' Her husband, who had popped out to get some cigarettes from the Railway Tavern, came in 'with his hair covered in debris'.

The disused school buildings, *c.* 1970 (CNT). In the winter of 1957, the new virulent strain of Asian flu played havoc with school attendance: in one week alone, 245 children were absent from the schools, 150 from the Junior School.

The top of St James Street at the junction with High Street and Bounty Street, *c.* 1975 (CNT). Geoff Lines' abiding memory as a pupil in the 1960s was being sent by the headmaster to the tobacconist's to buy him his Embassy cigarettes! The school was soon to close, however, and students were transferred to Radcliffe School in Wolverton.

The same St James Street junction, 1930s (CDC/Kitchener). The shop on the corner (left) has reportedly graduated over the years from a stable (complete with horse – 1900s), a draper's (1920s), a confectioner's and tobacconist's (1970s) to a barber's (1990s). Among other High Street shops which were fondly remembered were Lloyds' Fancy Goods and Wood's Sweet Shop. The boy looking at the camera is thought to be the photographer's son, David Kitchener.

The same junction, 1997 (MH).

High Street at the junction with Church Street, *c.* 1950 (MKM). The High Street was the main site of the LNWR cottages (seen right) demolished by WUDC. Three of the houses at the west end of the street had already been hit by a bomb in October 1940. The local news report, coyly mindful of the need for national security, noted only that 'a street' had been hit, though the details were more graphic: 'The first bomb fell in an allotment a few yards from a school. . . . The second was an oil-bomb that fell by the allotment fencing and splashed its contents against the wall of adjacent houses. This bomb was promptly treated with sand by two ladies . . . (the third) bomb scored a direct hit on two working-class houses . . . both were demolished, a third partly so . . .'.

There were five fatalities – four of them evacuees from London, two women and two children. The fifth was an elderly resident, George Bardell, aged 82. Geoff Lines recalled the story of a baby from one of the demolished houses: she was thrown by the force of the blast into Dr Love's garden on the other side of the street, and survived! One casualty, a housewife, was pulled out from under the table which had saved her life.

Pryke's the Milliner's was a notable shop in the street: one lad who learned his trade there before the First World War was Ernest Brandon. He joined up with the 7th Ox/Bucks Infantry in 1914 and survived the full four years of the war, mostly in Salonika. On his return, he became manager of the Wolverton Co-op at New Bradwell, but he died in 1937 from pneumonia, at the age of 42. Tom Blunt remembers the shop during the First World War selling replacement cellulite boys' collars when the old ones were cracked.

The same junction, 1930s (CDC/Kitchener). Mr and Mrs Joseph Burnham of 12 High Street received the news of their only son's death, at 21 years of age, in May 1915. This was one of three New Bradwell deaths reported by the *Wolverton Express* in one week alone: from 1 Spencer Street, Sergeant Adams, 'who would have been 20'; and Sergeant Edwin Gascoyne whose 'widow and little boy' had only recently moved into 39 Bridge Street. The 'Roll of Honour' column was a sad weekly fixture in the paper throughout the war.

The same junction, 1997 (MH).

This is believed to be the Co-op Procession, an annual event, seen at the west end of the High Street, *c.* 1910 (MKM). The pillars on the left show the entrance to Dr Love's garden – where the baby girl was blown by the 1940 bomb.

The west end of the High Street, 1997 (MH).

High Street from the east end, *c.* 1930 (BCC).

High Street from the east end, 1997 (MH). The green space in front of Permayne has replaced the railway cottage terraces.

Glyn Street at the junction with High Street, 1906 (WDAS). Glyn Street was named after George Carr Glyn, the London and Birmingham Railway Chairman from 1837 to 1853. He rode with Robert Stephenson to Birmingham on the first through-train journey in September 1838: 'Processions, parades, speeches, bands, flags and bunting . . . were seen at every station.' He became the 1st Baron Wolverton in 1869. 'The Board of Directors led by George Carr Glyn . . . really cared for the hundreds (they) employed and the thousands who depended on them for their health, education, and even places of worship' (Markham).

Payment certificate for two pigs reared by Bert Breedon, 1946 (MKM). One of the shops at the top of the street was Wylie's Butcher's. Like every butcher, it incorporated a slaughterhouse. If a pig was killed, the bladder was thrown to the kids, who blew it up and hit each other with it. They would also help with the slaughtering: 'There was a hole in the wall. The butcher would put a rope through. It was tied round the bullock's head. Then he told us kids to pull it as hard as possible to pull the head near the hole. Then he'd poleaxe it' (Hawtin Mundy).

A distinctive view of the railway cottages, *c.* 1965 (CDC/CNT). Seen from Church Street and shortly before demolition, the LNWR cottages stretch across High Street, Spencer Street and, at the top of the road, Bridge Street. Here is an excellent example of the hierarchical and ordered nature of Victorian industrial society: the small red-brick two-storey terraces were for the workers, with the three-storey pavilion end-terraces for the foremen. Each plot was 8 × 16 yards – thought to be very spacious for the time. Fireplaces were set in the corner with a cooking range in the kitchen. This would be black-leaded every morning, with the hearth whitened, the front step scrubbed, the pavement washed, the front-room fireplace polished with Brasso, and the steel fire-irons rubbed with emery paper.

The renovated Spencer Street, June 1987 (CNT). The present-day short, pedestrianised Spencer Street, named after Earl Spencer who controlled the parish of Stantonbury, is all that now remains.

The original Spencer Street, looking east, *c.* 1965 (CDC/CNT). Spencer Street ran parallel to the full length of the High Street. One of its shops – Sayells' – sold fish and chips. The fish came directly from Grimsby merchants, iced in boxes, sent by rail to Bradwell station. It was fried in the back yard and sold for 2*d.* The shop closed in 1940. You could also buy faggots and peas from Hepworth's, bread from Moore and Pierce, and everything else from Skrivener's General Stores. Tom Blunt remembers the neighbourliness of living at no. 42: 'If anyone was ill, they'd go and get her washing and do it, peel the potatoes, put dinner on and so on.'

Spencer Street, looking west, 13 September 1971 (CNT). One Spencer Street family suffered terribly during the First World War: in September 1917, the parents of Private James Morby learned of his death – their second son to be killed in the trenches; a third son had been so badly injured that his leg had been amputated. Twenty years later, however, there was cause for celebration at no. 31: Mr and Mrs Boddy celebrated their Golden Wedding, having been resident in the same house for 43 years. Mr Boddy could remember starting work at 7 years of age in 1865: he earned 1*s* 6*d* for a seven-day week on a farm. He later went to the works at Wolverton.

Spencer Street cleared for the Permayne development (left), March 1975 (CDC/CNT). At the start of the Second World War, 46 New Bradwell men had signed up, among them two from the Levitt family and the two Millard brothers – all from Spencer Street. Both Millards were reported missing in 1940, but were later found in a POW camp.

Spencer Street, 1997 (MH). The railway cottages were listed Grade III by the DoE, and subject to a public enquiry in 1975. The last section of Spencer Street was saved from demolition, purchased by MKDC, improved and restored in 1978, and became known as the Rainbow Housing Co-operative. Local songwriters Neil Mercer and Lyn Dawes captured some of the spirit of the place in their lyric for the 'Rainbow' song:

> 'Shoulder to shoulder the houses stand round,
> Each one with stories to share,
> And the walls catch the sun and they echo the sound
> Of the lives of everyone there.
> With the voices of children to make it complete,
> There's nowhere else quite like this New Bradwell street –
> That's why Rainbow's the place where you feel that you really belong . . .'.

Bridge Street on Coronation Day, 1902 (WDAS). Bridge Street, near canal bridge no. 72, also originally ran parallel to the full length of the High Street.

Bridge Street Armistice Party, 1918 (MKM). In the First World War, the street mourned one of its most noted residents, Private A. Walters of no. 59, who 'died from severe wounds in Salonika, aged 35', in June 1917. He had been a talented member of the Stantonbury Football Club. A more fortunate resident was celebrated 30 years later, however: Mrs Catherine Hawkins of no. 74 had enjoyed 62 years of marriage in the same house until her death, in January 1947.

Bridge Street war-time queue, *c.* 1944 (WDAS). In 1939, in preparation for the war, a model 'family trench' was dug in a field adjoining Bridge Street, for inspection by the council; in October 1940, however, it was almost at the epicentre of an air raid: 'a basket of flares' was dropped at the western edge of the street, falling on the allotments – now the school playing field.

Bridge Street being demolished in 1974 (CDC/CNT). The railway cottages of Bridge Street were unique in the LNWR development in that they did not have the three-storey foreman's house at the end of each terrace; they too were demolished by WUDC between 1965 and 1975. Geoff Lines, who lived in no. 60, remembers moving out with some sadness as a teenager: 'It was lovely in them little streets . . .'. The last family to leave, surrounded by demolition works, were the Williams.

Bridge Street, 1997 (MH).

Looking down Bradwell Road from the Canal Bridge, *c.* 1910 (WDAS). Bridge Street (left) marked the eastern limit of the homes built by the LNWR, and ran into the northernmost part of Bradwell Road known as Canal Hill. In January 1891, the *Bucks Standard* reported a 'curious accident to a traction engine'. As the Whiting Bros engine, engaged in some work for Farmer Wylie, came over the bridge, its brakes failed. 'The ponderous machine went crashing down the hill at a terrible speed', and ended up within half a yard of a cottage tenanted by the Faux family. Mrs Faux in her kitchen 'was naturally much frightened', but apart from a severely damaged engine, no harm was done.

Bradwell Road, New Bradwell, *c.* 1930 (CDC/Kitchener). The tollgate house, built in 1816, was originally at the foot of the hill, at the junction with Newport Road. Later, this was known as Busby's Corner: Bert and Harry Busby sold cockles, mussels, oysters, shrimps, winkles and whelks from their cart; it also doubled up as a corpse-carrier when suicides or drunks were fished out of the canal. In 1939, Harry was fined 5*s* with £1 1*s* vet's fees for 'causing unnecessary suffering' to his roan pony which was pulling the cart while it was lame. He caused great mirth in the courtroom when he said that as he hadn't taken any money that day, they should 'have it out in fish!'

Bradwell Road, 1997 (MH). Harry Busby's sister also had some claim to local fame: when she died in 1947, she had lived in the same house – no. 29 – for 74 years. In February of the same year, the 'great freeze-up' with 22° of frost caused great difficulties on the hill. Omnibuses could not climb it, cyclists could not ride down it, and 'pedestrians clung desperately to railings to prevent themselves falling' (*Express*). The approach to Canal Hill was later levelled out, but at the cost of replacing the old rounded stone bridge with the current rectangular bricked one.

The New Inn, *c.* 1920 (WDAS). Near the top of the hill, by the canal and just past the 1936 New Life Baptist Church, is the New Inn, built in 1804. In 1828, tenanted by Mr Newman Willeat, it was advertised for sale with 'a large and commodious Wharf, Stables for 30 horses, Corn Granaries, Coke and Salt Houses, Pigsties, Brewhouse, Wash-house, other detached Offices and a large garden'. The house had 'a spacious Kitchen, Bar, large Dining-room, Back Kitchen with Pump and a good Well of water'. There was 'cellarage for 100 hogsheads' (50,000 gallons), and 'large airy bedrooms'. It was 'a most compact and desirable residence' especially with its 'Quarry of building and limestone'.

The New Inn, 1997 (MH). Despite the flattering description, the inn used to be nicknamed the 'War Office' because of its riotous reputation from the navvies who built the Newport railway line. In 1864, it was run by the robust William Millward; but even in 1904, when Tom Squires became landlord, he was told that if he couldn't throw his customers out through the door, he was to throw them through the window! It was thought then to be 'a poor old place', mainly used by boat people. Next door was a blacksmith's shop, 'and at the rear a field where a Mr Beckett used to break in colts' (Hector Derricutt).

The Grand Union Canal and the Old Bridge, looking east, *c.* 1930 (CDC/Kitchener). In August 1927, the *Wolverton Express* reported on quieter times – a fishing competition held on the canal from the New Inn to Wolverton. The results were not sensational. The winner (from 27 competitors) won with a catch of 5 ounces – from two fish! Anglers had better luck if they fished from the Ouse: Fred Moore of Bradwell caught a record 4½ pound barbell in 1892; and Reg Mynard could remember, until 1939, the river teeming with fish: dace, silver bream, bronze bream, roach 'in shoals, hunted by perch and good-sized pike and eels – a fisherman's dream!'

The New Bridge, looking east, *c.* 1950 (BCC). The Canal House, or Wharf Cottage, was home to the Overton family for 35 years. Mr Overton was a 'lengthsman', controlling the waters of the Grand Union Canal with sluice gates into the Bradwell Brook; he also mowed the tow-paths with a scythe, kept the hedges cut and mended leaks.

The Stantonbury 'Unity' Football Team, 1891/2 (MKM). Later, in the 1930s, the New Inn was home to the Rhythm Boys, a leading dance band in the district, led by Harry Ward; later still, it was used for training by the local football team, New Bradwell St Peter, or Stantonbury St Peters, or the Peters.

Aerial view of the New Bradwell area, 1977 (CNT). Newport Road skirts New Bradwell (left), with Bradville housing top right; the Grand Union Canal (centre) and the old railway (right) are both crossed by the Bradwell Road, with the windmill lower right.

The former canal bridge at New Bradwell, looking west, 1938 (BCC). The canal used to be called the Grand Junction but was combined with the Grand Union Company in 1929. From its birth in 1791 it was a vital commercial link between London and Birmingham and for local communities. In 1806 – a year after the aqueduct at Wolverton had been opened – locals watched bemused as a record load of 100 live sheep passed by from Northampton on their way to the London market, taking just over two days to complete their 95-mile journey.

The 'New Bridge', looking west, 1997 (MH). Sometimes, up to 16 horses would be towing a barge, with old tins or boots tied behind them to make them think they were accompanied! The main traffic was in coal – 150,000 tons of it by 1830. Sand, gravel, roadstone, bricks, manure, milk, coconut oil and ale would also be seen gliding serenely past. By the 1930s motorised engines were taking over from the horses – they were faster and could travel by night; but it was the success of the railways that tolled the knell of doom for commercial traffic on the canal.

Goodman's Yard by the canal, *c.* 1975 (CNT). Chipperfield Close was the site of Goodman's famous scrap metal yard. It contained, among its piles of old iron, deceased steam locomotives. 'There used to be two men who worked together there – one big and burly, Rupert Jackson, and the other small, 'Tut' Cook. On Sundays, 'Tut' delivered papers. When he got to the New Inn, he called in. Sometimes, when he'd had too much, Rupert Jackson would put him in his cart, deliver the papers and then take him back to the pub!' (Charles Sambrook). No fewer than nine Goodman brothers composed a renowned darts team to challenge the 'Maggots' of Wolverton. The competition spread, with more teams being formed – which culminated in the creation of the British Legion Darts League.

The view across to New Bradwell, 1930s (BCC). Goodman's Yard was built on Aunt Mary's field, where there used to be lime kilns. The limestone was quarried from a huge hole, later used for rubbish, and burnt there. Hawtin Mundy tells us, 'In the evening, if the breeze was blowing towards New Bradwell, and you stood on the station at Wolverton, you couldn't see Bradwell – it was under a blanket of smoke.' Forty tons of coal were unloaded there every week for the kilns – at £1 a ton; and 30 tons of lime were sent out. The work ceased shortly before the First World War.

The view from Wolverton's Station Bridge, 1997 (MH). Grafton Street (V6), seen at the bottom of the picture, now cuts through to the city centre. The windmill can still be seen top right.

Bradwell station, 27 August 1954. Next to Goodman's Yard was Bradwell station (where the redway is, directly south of Chipperfield Close). Its single platform served the 'Nobby' line – at 4 miles long, the shortest in the county. It joined Wolverton and Newport Pagnell, stopping at Bradwell and Linford. There were up to 15 trains a day each way – one engine at a time – taking 4 minutes to get from Bradwell to Wolverton and 10 minutes to Newport Pagnell.

Bradwell station, 1950 (MKM). Goodman's Yard can be seen top left. The first engine ran on the 'Nobby' line in 1865 when it hauled 17 wagons 'crammed with navvies' (Arthur Griggs). The line opened for public service in 1867 and ran for nearly 100 years. Among its first station masters was Henry Roddis (1887); among its last, Albert West, who served from 1949 to 1961. He issued and collected tickets, balanced accounts, cleaned the station and, in his spare time, would deliver parcels to the neighbouring community.

The last day of service at Bradwell station, 5 September 1964 (LAP). The inventory for the station is a marvellous snapshot of pre-Beeching British Railways: the waiting room had three chairs, a blind and a looking glass; the booking office had three chairs, an office lamp, fire grate, fender, fire irons, double-faced clock, ticket case with 75 tubes, dating press and type, a counter with drawers, a coal cellar, oil lamp, signal lamp, oil can and broom; and the platform had three lamps, a framed bye-law poster, a name board, signals, siding indicator and an elegant vertical wrought-iron water pump.

View of Bradwell station, looking east towards Newport Pagnell, 1954 (LAP).

The same view, 1997 (MH).

A famous picture postcard of Bradwell station, *c*. 1910 (WDAS). Engine no. 58887, the LNWR tank engine arriving from Wolverton, worked on the 'Nobby' line for many years.

The old station platform, 1997 (MH). Looking west along the same stretch of the line, the cycle redway now runs to Wolverton. The last train left Bradwell station on 5 September 1964.

The old Baptist Church, operating as a shop, January 1975 (CNT). At one end of North Street, on the southern corner with Bradwell Road, the Baptist Chapel was built with a schoolroom incorporated in 1860. Later, it became an ironmonger's and general store; during the Second World War, it was a designated First Aid post.

The Baptist Church building, 1997 (MH).

New Bradwell Methodists, 1881 (BCC). On the corner with Thompson Street was the 'Prim' – the Primitive Methodist Chapel, built in 1865, where Hawtin Mundy went to Sunday School: 'Very, very good. They entertained you. During the week, they'd have a little concert party, and a Magic Lantern Show with slides of the Middle East; we'd laugh when the slides were put in upside down!' Sometimes, they joined the Baptists for outings on Lighthorn's barge: 'We'd go to Woolstone, have tea and a sing-song – enjoy ourselves beautiful!'

The Salvation Army Band, c. 1910 (MKM). In 1947, Charlie Daniels, of 9 Harwood Street, celebrated 50 years of service with the Salvation Army. For 40 of them, he said, he had visited 30 pubs every week, and had never had a drink! Half of the street was owned by Dr Miles, son-in-law of the first priest of New Bradwell, the Revd Cotter. Bradwell's most famous doctor, he had his own brougham driven by a cabman and wore a silk hat, frock-coat and tails. He also owned West View and the windmill.

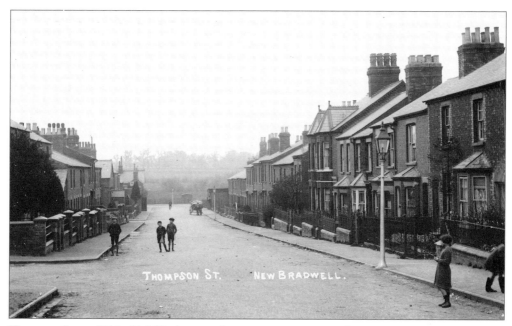

Thompson Street, 1930 (CDC/Kitchener). Thompson Street was named in 1856 after one of the LNWR directors. In 1893, the original Salvation Army Citadel was built there. Known as the Old Mill, it later moved to Newport Road. Thompson Street residents fought hard to save their houses at a public enquiry in October 1966 over living conditions: WUDC said that with their flooded cellars and damp rooms, they were not fit for human habitation. The owners maintained they could easily be put right. At the time, they lost the fight, and their houses became part of the first phase of compulsory purchase by the council, prior to demolition.

Thompson Street, 1997 (MH). Just off Thompson Street are Stantonbury Close, named after the abandoned village which preceded New Bradwell, and Bridgeway. An old swing-bridge over the canal used to be directly opposite the end of this road. It was thought Farmer Wylie's famous beef herds were driven over it on their way to the pasture at Stanton Low. In June 1957, excavations on the nearby canal bridge uncovered an old-fashioned lock-gate which acted like a drawbridge: it was calculated that it had not been used for over 100 years.

St Peter's Church, 1944 (BCC). A 1970s development which mostly rehoused residents of the railway cottages demolished by WUDC, St Peters Way is named after the 12th-century St Peter's Church a mile and a half away, the sole relic of the ancient village of Stanton Low. St Peter's fell into disuse in 1857 when the New Bradwell Church of St James was built.

The interior of St Peter's at the turn of the century (LAP). In 1903, the site of the old Manor House at St Peter's was reported still to be visible 'with its terraces and bowling green'. The church, too, still had its 'Jacobean oak pulpit and altar rails, its stone bench and Norman doorway'. It had become a local curiosity, a pause on the popular circular walk to Haversham: 'In the gable there is a single sanctus bell behind a curious little doorway.' The ancient helmet, sword, mask and gauntlets of Sir John Temple hung on the wall until 1944. Thereafter, with fires and looting, the church fell into disrepair, although the helmet and mask – seen on the wall in this picture – turned up in St James's Church in 1947.

A picture postcard of one of the 1909 weddings at St Peter's (LAP). The church became famous throughout the country in April 1909. The *Express* reported in its Easter edition on the first marriages to be solemnised at the church for half a century, following the Revd 'Joey' Guest's discovery that St James's had never been licensed for weddings. Hundreds of spectators lined the tow-path and track to the church. They 'sat on the jagged stones of the church wall, they reclined against the crumbling tombs, settled themselves in parties on the overgrown graves, and rested in laughing masses on the long green ridges that Cromwell threw over the demolished home of the monks'.

Mr and Mrs George Pedder after their wedding, 10 April 1909. Many people stayed after the ceremony to admire the old church with its 'Saxon doorway, famous all over England, the Norman pillars and arch, the old carved oak pulpit, and the flagstones of Saxon fashioning on which the bride and bridegroom knelt. Those well versed in the lore of the Church told the history of the knightly Tyrells, and the helmet, glove and sword of the ancient Lord of the Manor' (*Express*).

St Peter's, 1950s (BCC). Next to the old church, there used to be the railway company's Rifle Butts, or Stantonbury Range, built in 1879 for the use of the Rifle Volunteer Corps – later the Territorials. They provided much target practice for men soon to meet their fate in the trenches of the First World War. They were pulled down by Taylor's traction steam engines of Little Linford in 1927.

Service at St Peter's, Stanton Low, 1950s (LAP). The disused church buildings finally collapsed in 1957 and are now just a pile of ruins. However, its 12th-century chancel arch survived – by being removed to New Bradwell's (newly licensed) St James's Church and fixed over the west door.

St Peter's Church interior at Stanton Low, *c.* 1909 (CDC/CNT). Guest Gardens is named after the Revd 'Joey' Newman Guest, New Bradwell's best-known vicar. 'An Irishman with a keen sense of the dramatic', he announced one Sunday just after evensong that as 800 parishioners had married illegally in the unlicensed St James's since its opening in 1864, they were living in sin! Indeed, some respectable grandparents had been so doing for years. There was such local, and national, consternation that the Home Secretary himself had to make a special order validating all marriages.

Revd 'Joey' Guest, Vicar of St James's, 1908–46. Mr Guest died in 1946 after nearly 38 years at St James's during which time his forthright manner incited the vestry members to quarrel, the choir to strike and the congregation to leave in droves. William May remembered him as a huge man with a loud voice and 'very, very eccentric': he jogged barefoot and could leap five-bar gates. 'He had a phobia about flies. In summer, he covered his head in a paraffin-soaked handkerchief.' Bill Hood recalled how he used to ride his bicycle, sitting on a large motor-bike saddle, with his feet on specially made foot-rests just below the handlebars, shouting, 'Get out of the way!' Frank Harrap remembered being in the choir from the age of 8, even before Father Guest came. He thought he was 'a bold fellow. He believed in what he said. He could preach a sermon, never had no notes. It all came from his mouth. Wonderful really.' Hawtin Mundy tells of how 'whenever you met him on a Sunday evening when out for a stroll, he'd get off his bike and have quite a nice chat with you. He was greatly missed.'

SOURCES

Maurice Kitchener, *c.* 1930 (Mrs Kitchener).

The Kitchener Collection

The Kitchener Collection of around 2,000 glass plate negatives is a unique and precious resource in Milton Keynes. Not only do they record the former life and environs of local communities which, half a century later, were to be transformed into the UK's most dynamic and thriving new town; they also reveal the intricacies of a photographic process long since past. From the first ignition of magnesium powder (to light the subject) to the delicate procedures of printing (by shining sunlight through the glass plates onto special coated paper), the photographer had to be a master of timing and patience.

Maurice Kitchener, the middle son to an Olney factory owner, was born in 1894. Despite a few hindrances – like having to strap a wooden camera to his back and cycling to assignments – he became Newport Pagnell's most famous and respected photographer. His work covered the whole spectrum of local life: dances and parties, the subsequent weddings and consequent babies; farmers' prize bulls and gundogs; car factory production work (later to become the world-famous Aston Martin); corpses dragged from the canal; and pictures of gravestones for families grieving over lost loved ones.

However, perhaps the greatest significance of his work for Milton Keynes citizens is in the street scenes he shot in the 1920s and '30s specifically for sale as postcards in local shops. He developed and printed the postcards himself and employed his younger son, David, to deliver them around the villages. Many local books have since used these as a prime resource.

When his father died in 1969, David was determined to preserve his work and to record the singular life he had led. The former wish was fulfilled when the Collection went on permanent loan to the Milton Keynes City Discovery Centre, securing a safe and accessible resource for future generations. Sadly, David died in July 1997 before he could fulfil his latter wish: his father's biography remains unfinished. However, the author is very grateful to Mrs Kitchener for allowing some 16 of the plates to be used for this book: they are in themselves a continuing memorial both to father and son.

The Living Archive (LAP) (formerly the Living Archive Project)

The Living Archive has pioneered documentary arts work in Milton Keynes. It has inspired others throughout Britain and overseas to do similar work, listening to local people's histories and using them to inspire creative projects that celebrate the place where they live.

Established in 1984, The Living Archive has produced 11 large-scale documentary plays; 20 books of local reminiscence; radio documentaries; textile and mosaic projects; dance; tape/slide and video projects; exhibitions; interactive CD ROMs. In researching these projects, an archive of over 700 hours of taped reminiscence and over 10,000 slides, photographs and documents has been collected. Based at the Old Bath House in Wolverton, this archive is used by schools, university students and local people researching their family histories – and by the author who is indebted to Living Archive staff for their help, support, encouragement and accessibility.

Milton Keynes Museum of Industry and Rural Life (MKM)

The 'Stacey Hill Collection' of farm implements and rural artefacts was begun at its Wolverton farmhouse home in 1973, right at the beginning of the building programme for the new city of Milton Keynes. Despite a terrible fire which destroyed some irreplaceable items, it is due to open (Easter 1998) in new, purpose-built premises with an ever-increasing collection. It houses a unique newspaper archive as well as rooms furnished with authentic equipment and furniture – such as in a Victorian schoolroom. A popular resource for visiting schools, the museum gives enormous help to researchers – including the author who is most grateful.

The Wolverton and District Archaeological Society (WDAS)

Founded in 1955, the Society aims at making the general public more aware and appreciative of the story and history of the Wolverton locality. It also endeavours to see that listed buildings, historic objects and sites are preserved.

The Society organises monthly illustrated talks on topics as varied as 'The Leather Trade of Stony Stratford', 'The Railways and the Post' and 'Buildings around Milton Keynes at the time of the English Civil War'. It also organises guided walks, outings to places of interest and historical celebrations and dinners.

It preserves a photographic record of Old North Bucks, and now has 12,000 slides. It issues a newsletter and pamphlets, and publishes reprints of local history books. The author is very grateful for the Society's permission to use prints from its unique collection of slides; and particularly for the time and kind assistance of the Photographic Secretary, Ron Unwin.

The City Discovery Centre (CDC)

The Centre, based at Bradwell Abbey, has built up an extensive and varied collection of resources on the Milton Keynes area. Its Library covers such topics as Architecture and Urban Design, Local History and 'Green' issues; it has a wide collection of slides, photographs, maps and resource packs; and its facilities include study facilities and lecture rooms. The Kitchener Collection can be viewed there, or prints purchased at the centre. Staff are very helpful, for which the author is most appreciative.

The Commission for New Towns (CNT)

The Commission for New Towns (CNT) has inherited from the former Milton Keynes Development Corporation a vast collection of photographs and documents of the new city's development – before, during and after its transformation. Scrupulously catalogued and stored, the collection provides a priceless resource for researchers. The author is very grateful for the kindness and help of CNT staff for providing so many of the photographs for this book.

Buckinghamshire County Council (BCC)

Libraries have been an important source for this book. The author is particularly grateful to the County Records and Local Studies staff who gave access to, and loaned, their scarce resources.

ACKNOWLEDGEMENTS

In addition to the organisations described overleaf, the author would like to acknowledge the contribution made to this book by:

Living Archive transcripts of interviews with: Mr Baldwin, Eric Bellchambers, Tom Blunt, Frederick Church, Iris Davies, Hector Derricutt, Mr Dickens, A.N. Guest, Frank Harrap, Bill Hood, Ivy Johnson, William May, Hawtin Mundy, Percy Mundy, Charles Sambrook, Lily Stonton, Sidney Teagle, Frances Welch; the log books of the New Bradwell Schools, 1867–1946; and the diaries of Mrs Nellie Abbey (née Smith), 1901–1920.

Ray and Mary Bellchambers for sharing their vast knowledge of Bradwell, Old and New.

Geoff Lines for his impromptu memories of New Bradwell.

Harvest Studios at Linford Forum, especially Ian Douse, for their excellent photographic services.

Aerofilms for permission to use the photographs on pages 24 and 56.

Diane Duff and Doris Hill for help with proofing.

Bob Hill.

BIBLIOGRAPHY

Bellchambers and Mynard, *History of Bradwell, Bradwell Abbey, New Bradwell*, 1994

Bradwell Chapel pamphlet, 1986

M. Clarke, *Railway Cottages, Spencer Street*, 1979

Revd W. Cole: *Diaries*, 1766

M. Ehrenberg, *Bronze Age Spearheads from Berks, Bucks, & Oxon.*, 1977

C.F. Farrar, *The Ouse's Silent Tide*, 1952

M. Green, *The Bradwell Roman Villa*, MKDC, 1975

A. Griggs, *Country Railwaymen*, 1982

Harrods' Guide, 1876

J. Healy, *Last Days of Steam in Buckinghamshire*, 1989

Kelly's Directories, 1864, 1887, 1907

LMS Railway Route Book no. 2, *Along the Viking Border*, 1947

F. Markham, *The Nineteen Hundreds*, 1951

F. Markham, *History of Milton Keynes and District*, 1976

MKDC Archaeological Unit, *Windows on the Past*, 1992

D. Mynard, *Bancroft: Prehistoric Farm to Roman Villa*, MK Archaeological Unit, 1984

R. Mynard, *Memories in Milton Keynes*, 1984

Sheahan Guide, 1861

B. Simpson, *The Wolverton to Newport Pagnell Branch*, 1995

Victoria County History Volume 4

Paul Woodfield and MKDC, *A Guide to the Historic Buildings of Milton Keynes*, 1985